Saint Quotes on Love

Catholic Meditations Coloring Book

plus Note Cards to Color

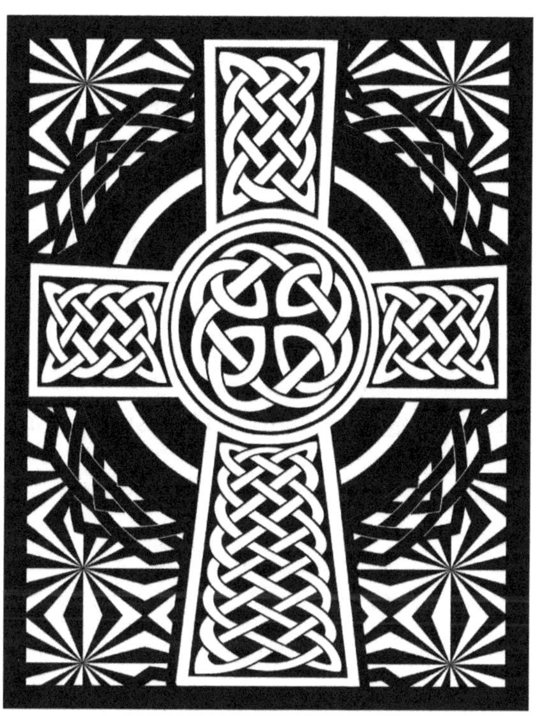

Kathryn Marcellino

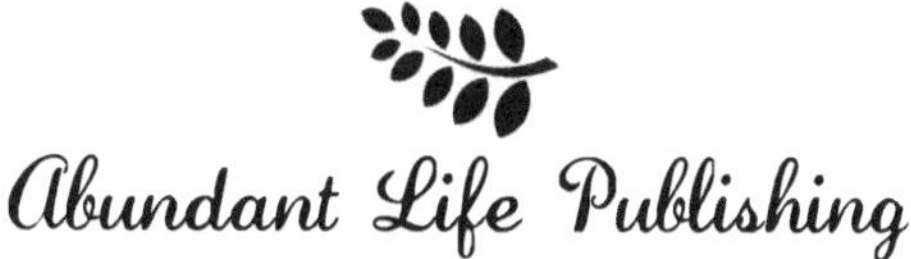

Abundant Life Publishing

Cover design, illustrations, and graphic design are by Kathryn Marcellino,
www.custom-graphic-design.com.

This book includes 30 full-size illustrations plus 22 note cards to color.

ISBN 978-1-944158-03-3 (Paperback)

Abundant Life Publishing
PO Box 3753
Modesto, CA 95352
email: km@AbundantLifePublishing.com

www.AbundantLifePublishing.com

Printed in the USA

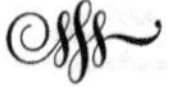

Other books by Kathryn Marcellino include:

Jesse Tree Ornaments: Advent Coloring Activities and Craft Projects for Kids with Bible Stories

Twenty Mysteries of the Rosary Coloring Book

Rosary Meditations: The Gospel in Miniature

Christian Cathedrals Stained Glass Coloring Book

Art Extensions Christian Art Masterpieces Drawing and Coloring Book

Table of Contents

About this Book

This is a Catholic coloring book for adults, teens, and older children. The simpler design of many of the illustrations and the short saint quotes also make it easy for busy people, as well as kids and senior citizens to color. The book makes a unique gift also for grandparents and the elderly and can be used as a quiet activity for the sick, disabled, and those in nursing homes, or assisted living as well. There are 30 full-page illustrations including religious art, floral designs, and other patterns to color. There are also 22 note cards to color, cut out, and give away.

One way to use this book is to reflect on the inspirational quotes from saints and the Bible while coloring inspirational art. The quotes by saints and from Sacred Scripture help set the mood for reflection and meditation on Jesus Christ and his teachings regarding the importance of love. Meditating on the quotations and coloring the pages helps lift the mind to heavenly things. Additional information for each featured quote is provided on the preceding page.

There are no rules on how to color, and you don't even need to stay in the lines. Feel free to use any colors or media you like such as crayons, colored pencils, felt-tip pens, or markers. The illustrations are printed on one side of the page on 60# library-quality, white paper. If using markers or paint, a sheet of paper may be inserted underneath the page while coloring to protect the next page. Copies may be made of the pages before coloring if desired. Coloring is a great way to relax and to express oneself artistically. Reflection helps put one's mind on God and helps prepare for prayer.

The following passage from Scripture refers to the coloring page to the right:

> 34 *When the Pharisees heard that he had silenced the Sadducees, they gathered*
> *together,* 35 *and one of them [a scholar of the law] tested him by asking,*
> 36 *"Teacher, which commandment in the law is the greatest?"* 37 *He said to him,*
> *"You shall love the Lord, your God, with all your heart, with all your soul, and*
> *with all your mind.* 38 *This is the greatest and the first commandment.* 39 *The*
> *second is like it: You shall love your neighbor as yourself.* 40 *The whole law and*
> *the prophets depend on these two commandments.*

Matthew 22:34-40
New American Bible, revised edition (NABRE)

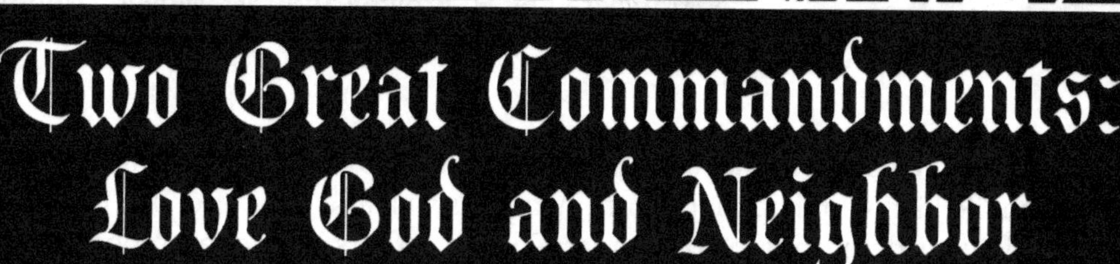

Two Great Commandments: Love God and Neighbor

You shall love the Lord your God with all your heart, with all your soul, and with all your mind.

You shall love your neighbor as yourself.

From Matthew 22:37-40

"Inasmuch as love grows in you, in so much beauty grows; for love is itself the beauty of the soul."

Saint Augustine of Hippo
From *The Nicene and Post Nicene Fathers*,
as translated by H. Browne and J. H. Meyers, (1995)

Saint Augustine of Hippo (354–430) was a theologian, writer, philosopher, Catholic bishop of Hippo in North Africa, as well as a Doctor of the Church. He is considered one of the Great Church fathers. His contemporary St. Jerome said that St. Augustine "established anew the ancient Faith."

As a young man Augustine was well educated and influenced by the secular philosophies of the time including Manichaeism and later the Neo-Platonism of Plotinus. He reached a point that he felt God was calling him to be a Christian, but he struggled with Christian teachings as he had a mistress and did not want to give up his sinful lifestyle. He even prayed, "Grant me chastity and continence, but not yet."

At the age of 31, he was inspired by hearing the story of the life of Saint Anthony of the Desert. One day while feeling torn and reflecting on his life, he began to weep under a tree and then heard a childlike voice saying, "take up and read". He understood this to mean that God was asking him to open the Bible and read the first thing he came to. He opened the Bible and read Romans 13:13-14, "...let us conduct ourselves properly as in the day, not in orgies and drunkenness, not in promiscuity and licentiousness, not in rivalry and jealousy. But put on the Lord Jesus Christ, and make no provision for the desires of the flesh."

In his book *Confessions,* he tells his personal story of his earlier life, sins, struggles, and conversion. This book is considered a Christian classic and also includes philosophical topics such as the nature of time and free will. Below is one passage from this book:

Late have I loved Thee, O Lord; and behold,
Thou was within and I without, and there I sought Thee.
Thou was with me when I was not with Thee.
Thou didst call, and cry, and burst my deafness.
Thou didst gleam, and glow, and dispel my blindness.
Thou didst touch me, and I burned for Thy peace.
For Thyself Thou hast made us,
And restless our hearts until in Thee they find their ease.
Late have I loved Thee, Thou Beauty ever old and ever new.

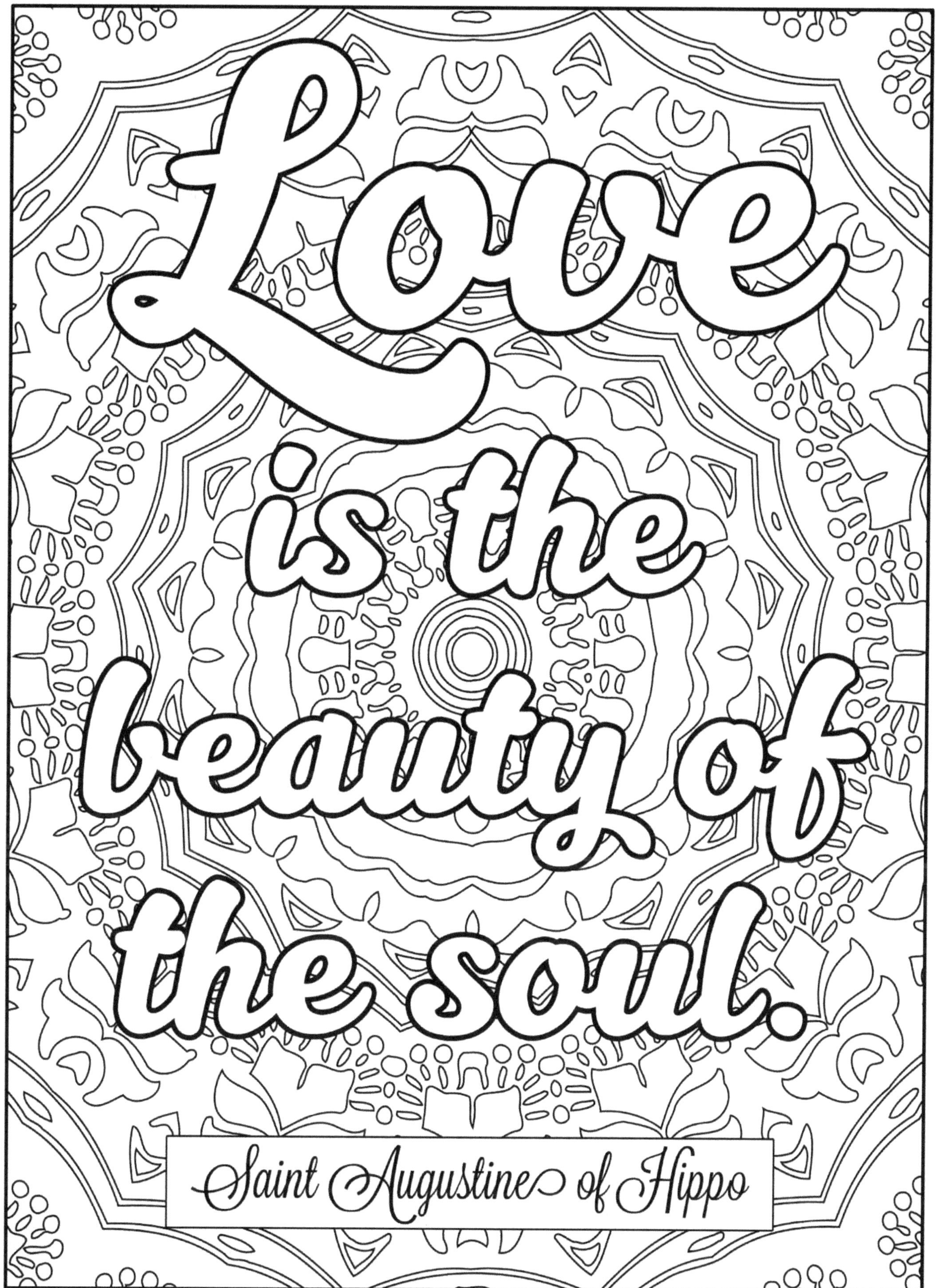
Love
is the
beauty of
the soul.
Saint Augustine of Hippo

"Pure love is capable of great deeds, and it is not broken by difficulty or adversity. As it remains strong in the midst of great difficulties, so too it perseveres in the toilsome and drab life of each day."

Saint Faustina Kowalska
From the *Diary of Saint Faustina*
www.divinemercy.org

Saint Maria Faustina Kowalska of the Blessed Sacrament (1905–1938) was a young nun from a poor family in Poland who had only a few years of simple education. She struggled to be able to join the Congregation of Sisters of Our Lady of Mercy and was assigned the simplest tasks. She received messages and visions from Jesus, who revealed to her the power of God's mercy towards all people, but especially towards those most in need of God's compassionate love. Jesus said that he wanted all people to put their trust in him and never to despair or doubt that he will forgive sins if people are repentant, no matter how horrible the sins. Jesus asked her to have a painting made of an image of Jesus that was revealed to her to help establish devotion to Divine Mercy. Saint Faustina and her confessor Father Michal Sopoćko directed an artist to paint the first Divine Mercy image, which at the bottom says, "Jesus, I trust in you." Sopoćko used this painting in celebrating Mass on the first Sunday after Easter. Later Pope John Paul II established the Feast of Divine Mercy on that Sunday of each year. St. Faustina was instructed to record her experiences, which is called *The Diary of Saint Maria Faustina Kowalska: Divine Mercy in My Soul.* This amazing work sparked a great movement focusing on God's endless mercy, and for all to be merciful to others. St. Faustina was canonized in the year 2000.

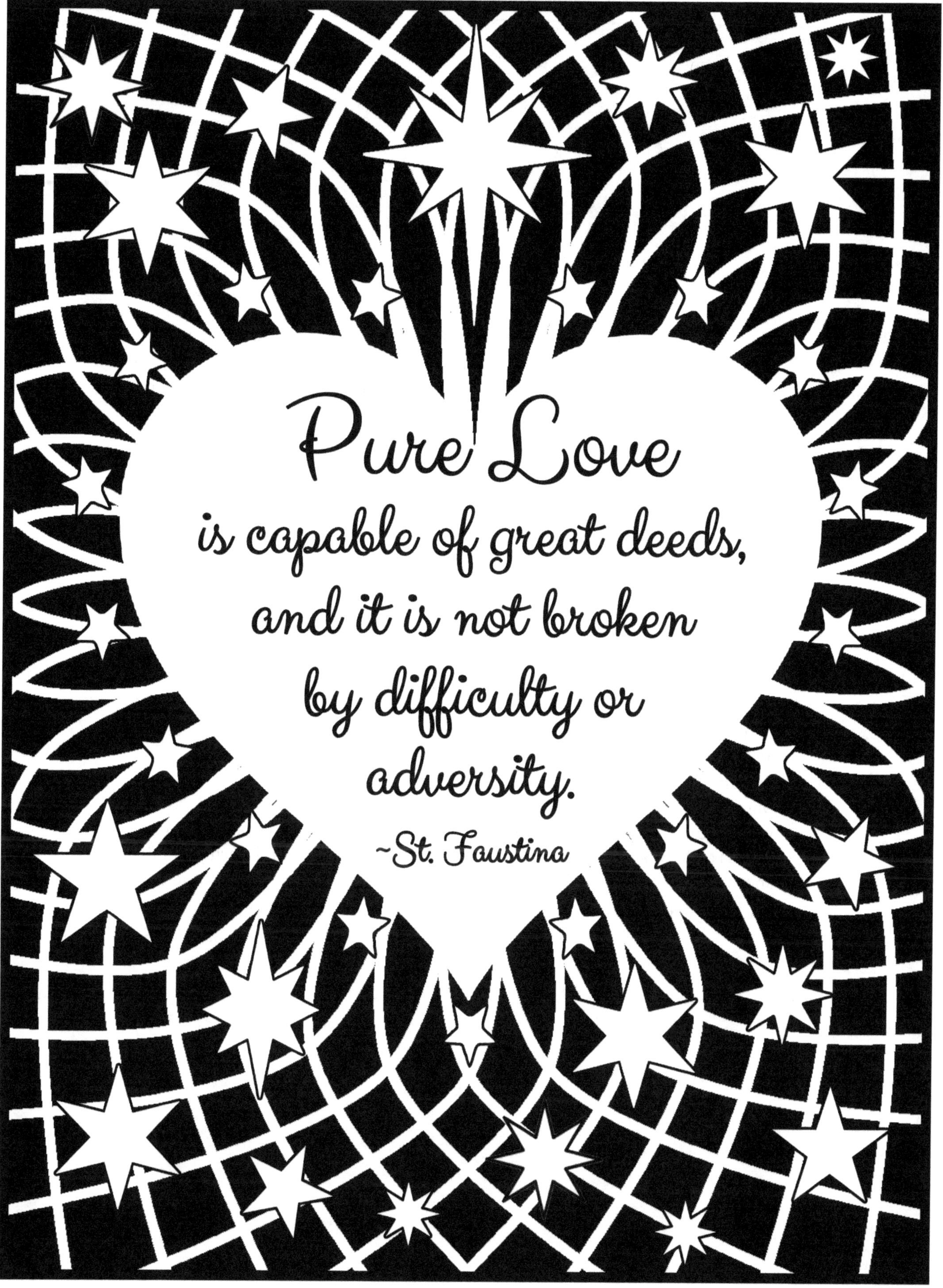
Pure Love
is capable of great deeds,
and it is not broken
by difficulty or
adversity.
~St. Faustina

"Spread love everywhere you go; first of all in your own house. Give love to your children, to your wife or husband, to a next door neighbor. Let no one ever come to you without leaving better and happier. Be the living expression of God's kindness; kindness in your face, kindness in your eyes, kindness in your smile."

Saint Teresa of Calcutta (Mother Teresa)
As quoted in *Worldwide Laws of Life: 200 Eternal Spiritual Principles* (1998)
by John Templeton, p. 448

Mother Teresa, now known as Saint Teresa of Calcutta (1910 –1997), was an Albanian nun and missionary to India. In 1950 Teresa founded the Missionaries of Charity, a religious congregation, which by 2012 had grown to having over 4,500 sisters spread throughout 133 countries. The sisters manage homes for people dying of various diseases including AIDS, leprosy, and tuberculosis. They also have soup kitchens to help feed the poor, dispensaries, clinics, counseling programs, orphanages, and schools. Members take vows of chastity, poverty, and obedience, and also a fourth vow to give "wholehearted free service to the poorest of the poor". Mother Teresa's life was an example of Christian love and service, and during her life she was regarded as a living saint. She was canonized by Pope Francis on September 4, 2016.

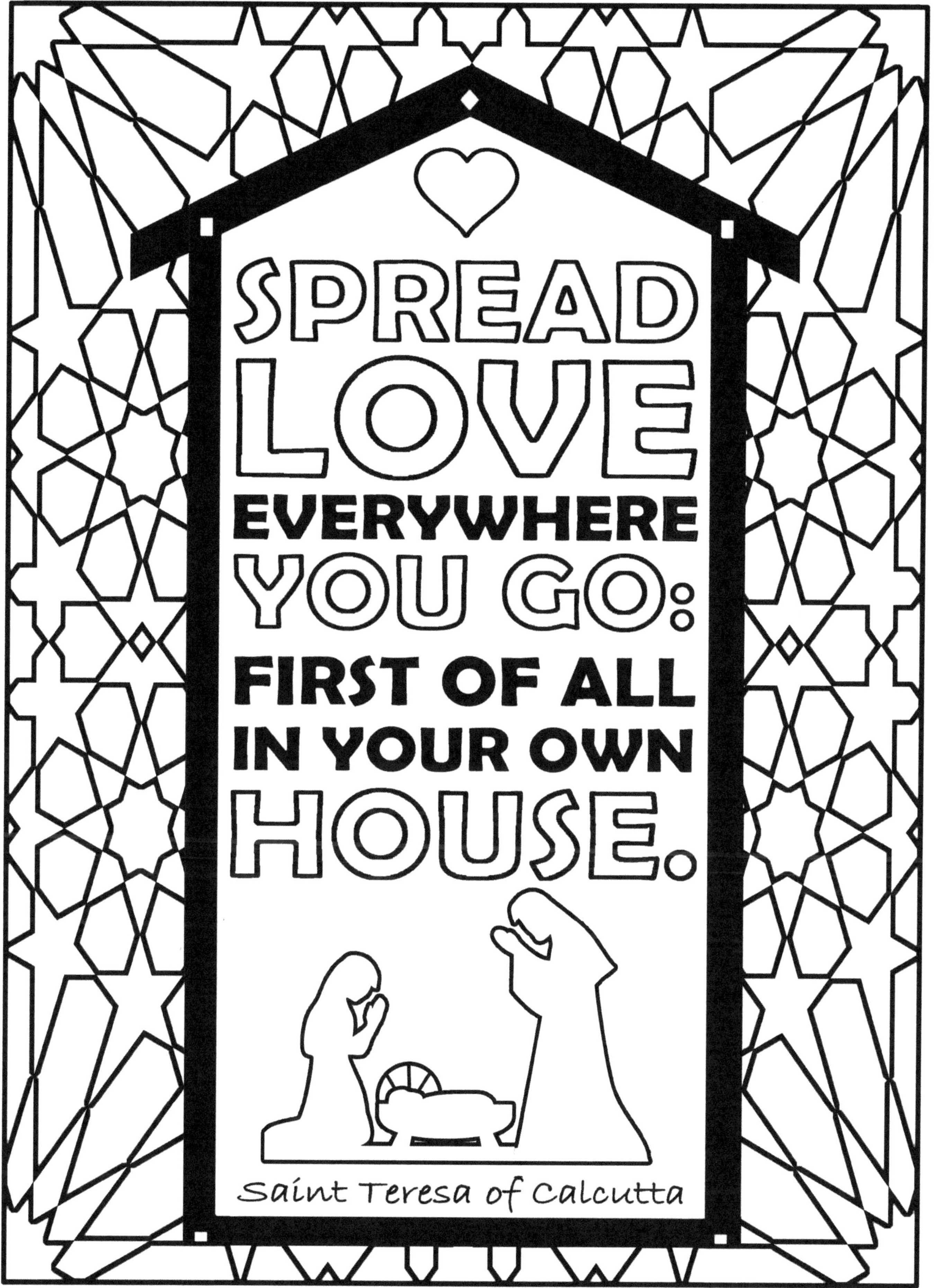
SPREAD
LOVE
EVERYWHERE
YOU GO:
FIRST OF ALL
IN YOUR OWN
HOUSE.
Saint Teresa of Calcutta

*1 If I speak in human and angelic tongues but do not have love, I am a
resounding gong or a clashing cymbal. 2 And if I have the gift of prophecy and
comprehend all mysteries and all knowledge; if I have all faith so as to move
mountains but do not have love, I am nothing. 3 If I give away everything I own,
and if I hand my body over so that I may boast but do not have love, I gain
nothing. 4 Love is patient, love is kind. It is not jealous, [love] is not pompous,
it is not inflated, 5 it is not rude, it does not seek its own interests, it is not
quick-tempered, it does not brood over injury, 6 it does not rejoice over
wrongdoing but rejoices with the truth. 7 It bears all things, believes all things,
hopes all things, endures all things.*

1 Corinthians 13:1-7
New American Bible, revised edition (NABRE)

⇨

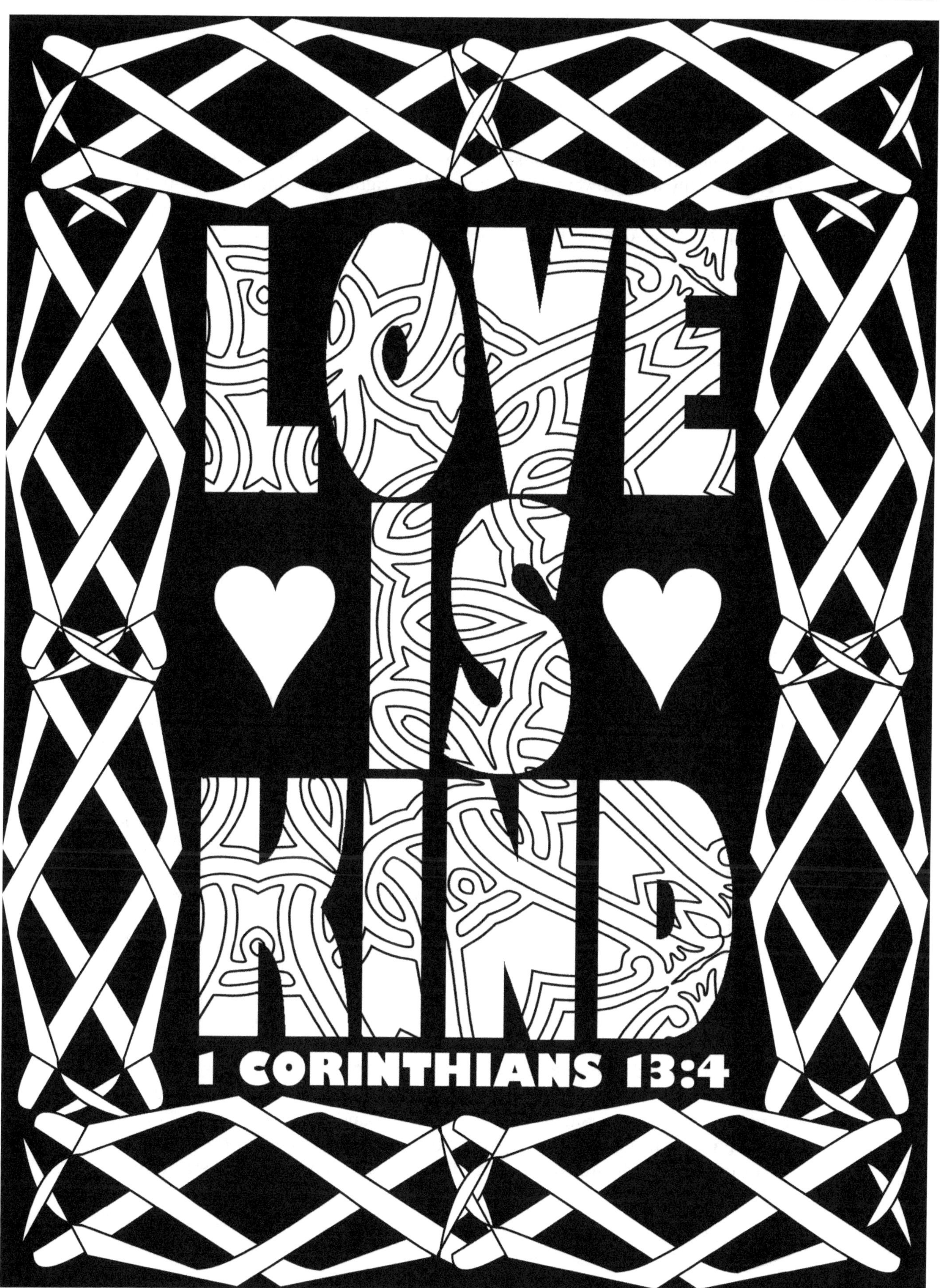
LOVE
IS
KIND
I CORINTHIANS 13:4

Some sayings of Saint Thérèse de Lisieux regarding love:

"Miss no single opportunity of making some small sacrifice, here by a smiling look, there by a kindly word; always doing the smallest right and doing it all for love."

"For me, prayer is a surge of the heart; it is a simple look turned toward heaven, it is a cry of recognition and of love, embracing both trial and joy."

"Without love, deeds, even the most brilliant, count as nothing."

"When I die, I will send down a shower of roses from the heavens, I will spend my heaven by doing good on earth."

"I know now that true charity consists in bearing all our neighbors' defects— not being surprised at their weakness, but edified at their smallest virtues."

Saint Thérèse of Lisieux (1873–1897) was a Discalced Carmelite nun. Her religious name was **Thérèse of the Child Jesus and the Holy Face**. She is popularly known as "The Little Flower". Pope Pius X called her "the greatest saint of modern times".

Thérèse had a simple and practical approach to the spiritual life called the "Little Way" of spiritual childhood. She put great confidence and love in God as a little child does to a loving earthly father for all her needs including her desires to be holy. She said, "I wanted to find an elevator that would raise me to Jesus." The elevator she was speaking of was the arms of Jesus lifting her up despite or even because of her littleness.

As a child, Thérèse felt called to be a nun. She was influenced to love and follow Jesus by her saintly parents. Her older sisters had entered the convent, and Therese also wanted to enter religious life. She was told she was too young and even made a trip to see the pope to ask to enter earlier than generally allowed. Eventually at the early age of 15, she was allowed to join her two older sisters in the cloistered Carmelite community of Lisieux, France. She lived there for nine years and had various duties including assistant to the novice mistress but fell ill with tuberculosis. Her last year and a half were filled with suffering both physical and spiritual, and she died at the age of 24. Her last words were, "My God, I love you!"

She had been asked before her death to write her story called *The Story of a Soul*. This was distributed after her death, and she has become one of the most popular saints in modern times. She was beatified in 1923 and canonized in 1925. In 1997, Pope John Paul II declared her a Doctor of the Church. She was the thirty-third Doctor of the Church, and also the third woman and the youngest person to ever receive this title.

It is love
alone
that counts.
~St. Therese of Lisieux,
The Little Flower

"A soul enkindled with love is a gentle, meek, humble, and patient soul."

Saint John of the Cross
Sayings of Light and Love, #29

Two more sayings of St. John of the Cross about love:

"A soul that walks in love neither rests nor grows tired."

"At the end of our life, we shall all be judged by charity."

Saint John of the Cross (1542–1591) was a Spanish mystic, a Discalced Carmelite friar, and a priest. He was a friend of St. Teresa of Avila and was cofounder with her of the Discalced Carmelite order, which is a reform of the original Carmelite order. He is known for his writings including *The Ascent of Mount Carmel* and *Dark Night of the Soul.* His writings are considered to be some of the greatest writings in the Church on the growth in the spiritual life, union with God, and mysticism. John of the Cross taught that the soul must empty itself of self and other things in order to be filled with God. He was canonized in 1726 and later named the thirty-sixth Doctor of the Church.

A soul enkindled with love is a gentle, meek, humble, and patient soul.

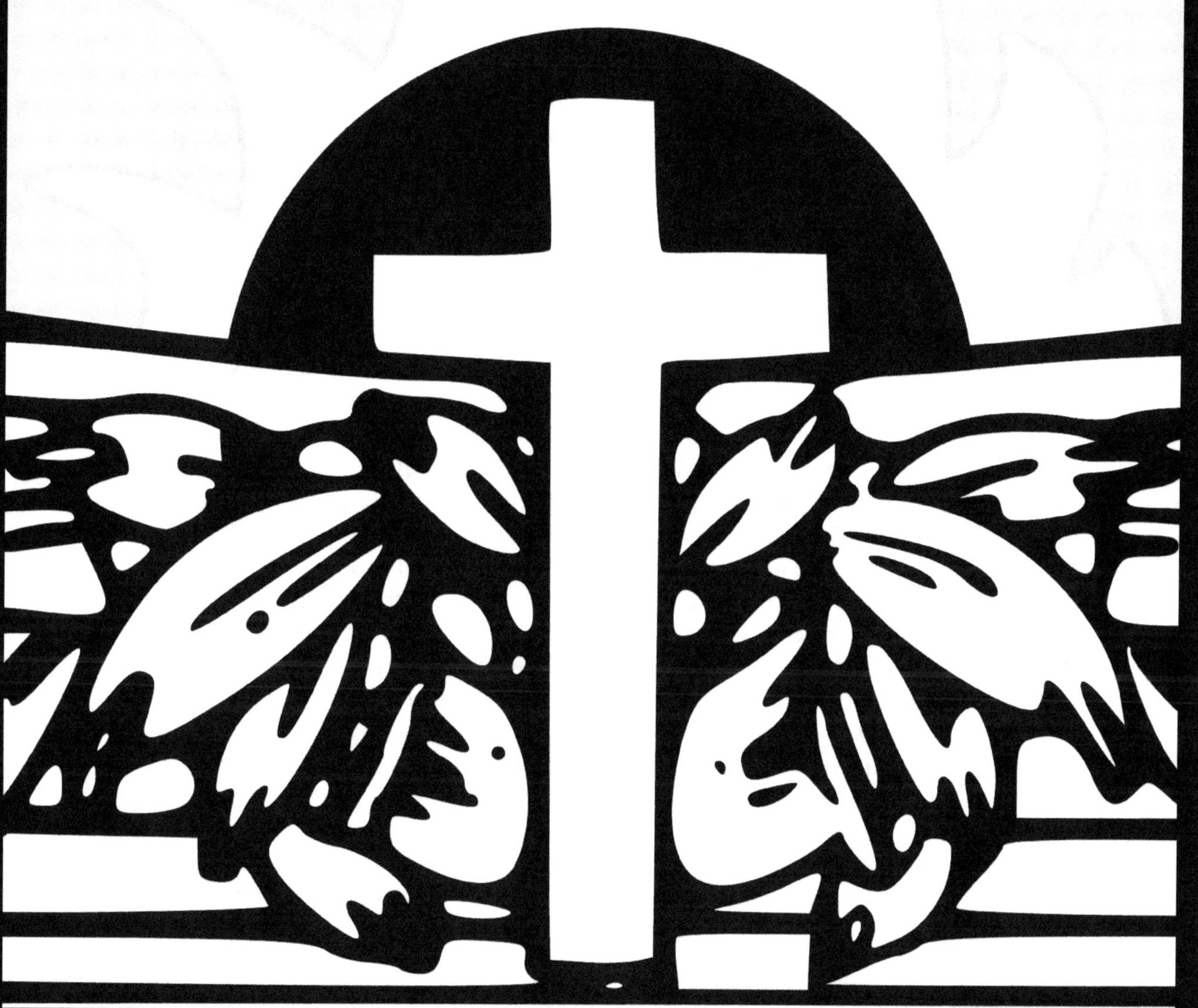

St. John of the Cross, OCD

" 'We know that in everything God works for good for those who love him.' The constant witness of the saints confirms this truth: Saint Catherine of Siena said to 'those who are scandalized and rebel against what happens to them': 'Everything comes from love, all is ordained for the salvation of man, God does nothing without this goal in mind.' "

Catechism of the Catholic Church #313

Saint Catherine of Siena (1347–1380), was a lay member of the Dominican order and the second woman to be proclaimed a Doctor of the Church. She was the youngest of a large family. From early childhood she saw visions and practiced extreme austerities. She consecrated her virginity to Christ at age seven and at age sixteen became a Dominican tertiary and spent most of her time in her room at home in prayer. After three years of celestial visitations and conversation with Christ, she underwent the mystical experience known as the "spiritual espousals". She then rejoined her family, began to tend the sick, serve the poor, and labor for the conversion of sinners. She suffered terrible physical pain and lived for long intervals on practically no food except the Blessed Sacrament, but she was ever happy and full of practical wisdom with the highest spiritual insight. She received a series of special manifestations of Divine mysteries, which culminated in a prolonged trance, a kind of mystical death, in which she had a vision of Hell, Purgatory, and Heaven, and heard a Divine command to leave the solitude of her room and enter the public life of the world. She began to dispatch letters to men and women in every condition of life, entered into correspondence with the princes and republics of Italy, was consulted by the papal legates about the affairs of the Church, and set herself to heal the wounds of her native Italy torn by civil war. She implored Pope Gregory XI to leave Avignon, France, to reform the clergy and the administration of the Papal States, and to work toward restoring peace to Italy. She miraculously learned to write, though she still seems to have chiefly relied upon her secretaries for her correspondence and at one point dictating her *Dialogue*, the book of her meditations and revelations. (Adapted from *The Catholic Encyclopedia*, 1913 edition.)

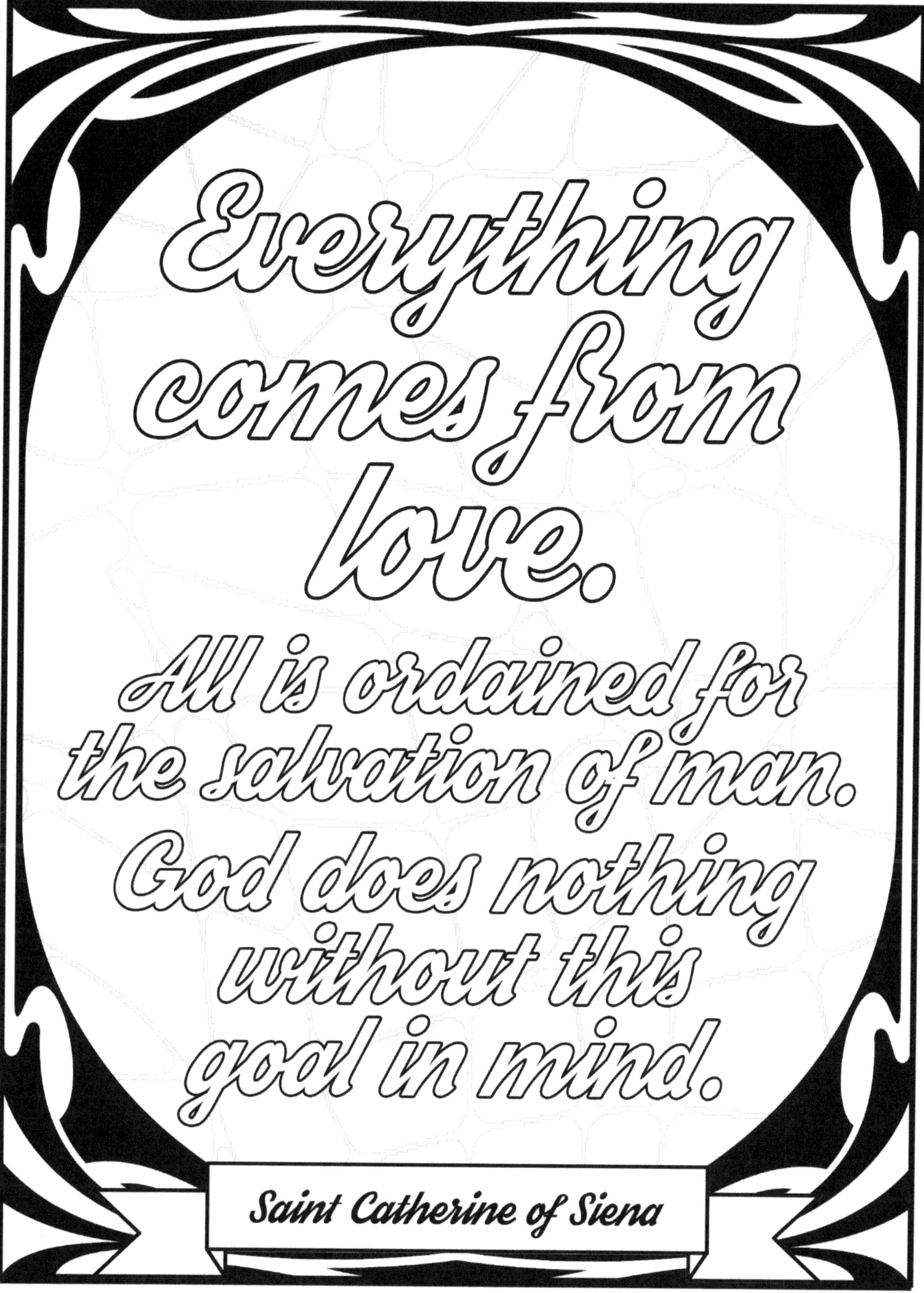
Everything comes from love.
All is ordained for the salvation of man.
God does nothing without this goal in mind.
Saint Catherine of Siena

“There is no place for selfishness and no place for fear! Do not be afraid when love makes demands. Do not be afraid when love requires sacrifice.”

Pope Saint John Paul II

Pope Saint John Paul II (1920–2005) born Karol Wojtyła was pope from 1978 to 2005. He is sometimes called Saint John Paul the Great because of his great holiness and accomplishments. He became the 264th pope and the first non-Italian pope in 455 years. Over his long pontificate he named many of the Cardinals and consecrated many bishops. He wrote 14 papal encyclicals and is also known also for his writings on the meaning of sexuality called the “Theology of the Body”. John Paul also ordered the publication of the *Catechism of the Catholic Church* and called it “a sure norm for teaching the faith . . . a sure and authentic reference text for teaching Catholic doctrine and particularly for preparing local catechisms”.

He received his priestly formation and training in his native country Poland in secret because of the oppressive occupation first by Nazi Germany during World War II and then the USSR. Later as pope, he was instrumental in helping to end Communist rule by being the spiritual inspiration behind “a peaceful revolution” in Poland. While pope, he travelled more extensively than previous popes to over 100 countries. He beatified 1,340 people and canonized 483 saints, which is more than the total for the past five centuries.

Pope John Paul II took as his apostolic motto, *Totus Tuus,* which means “completely yours” to which he entrusted himself to the Blessed Mother Mary as his spiritual mother. Later he would credit Mary’s intercession for saving his life when Mehmet Ali Agca, a Turkish gunman, shot him on May 13, 1981, the feast day of Our Lady of Fatima. Even though he was seriously wounded, he survived and later said, "It was a mother's hand that guided the bullet's path." One of the bullets that hit him was placed in the crown of the status of the Blessed Mother at Fatima, Portugal.

Pope John Paul II lived a life of prayer, work, charity, and heroic virtue, and was an inspiration to many. He died on the vigil of the feast of Divine Mercy, a feast he had established as pope, and was canonized by Pope Francis on Divine Mercy Sunday, April 27, 2014 along with Pope John XXIII.

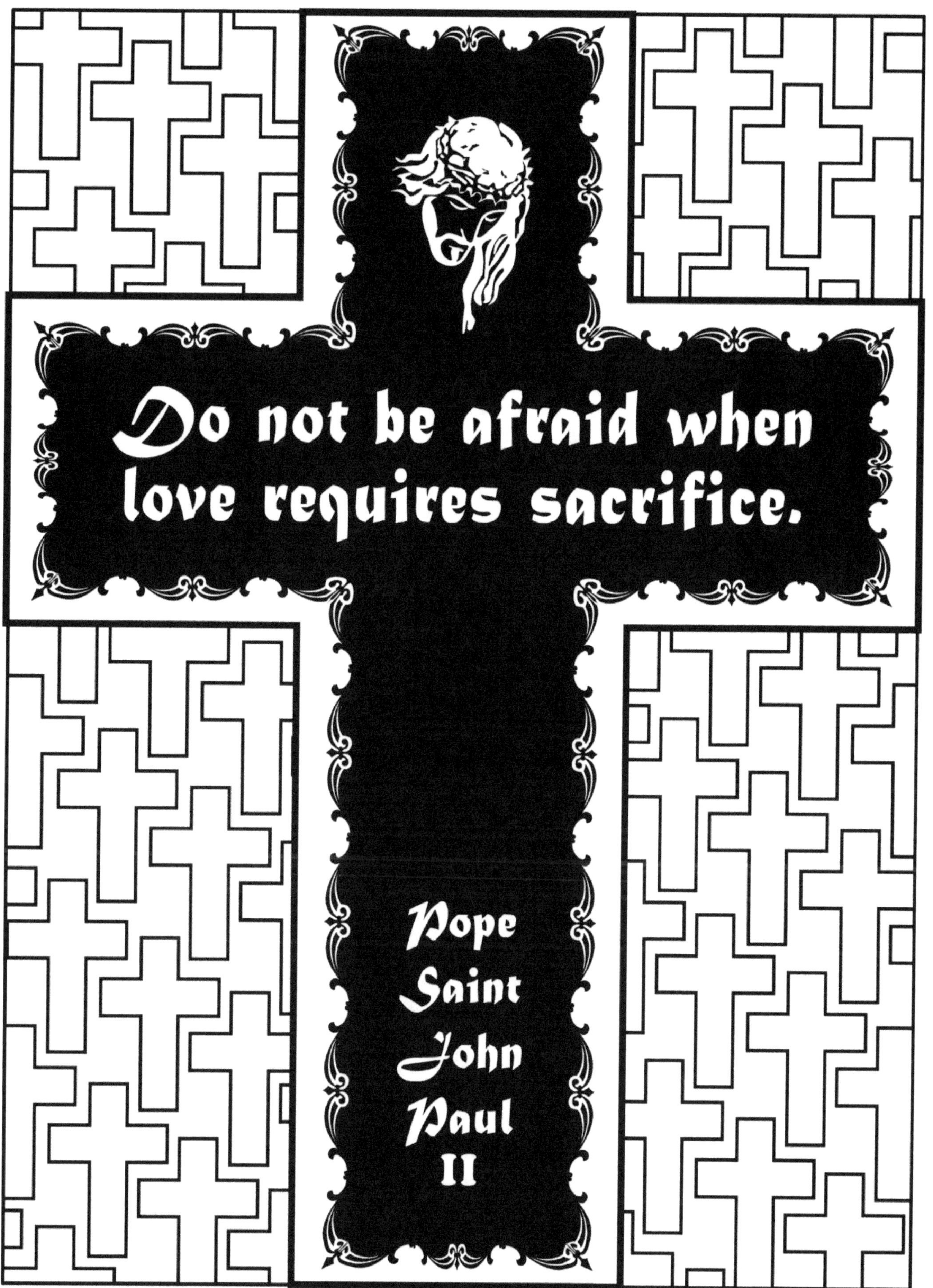
Do not be afraid when
love requires sacrifice.
Pope
Saint
John
Paul
II

[8] Love never fails. If there are prophecies, they will be brought to nothing; if tongues, they will cease; if knowledge, it will be brought to nothing. [9] For we know partially and we prophesy partially, [10] but when the perfect comes, the partial will pass away.

1 Corinthians 13:8-10
New American Bible, revised edition (NABRE)

⇨

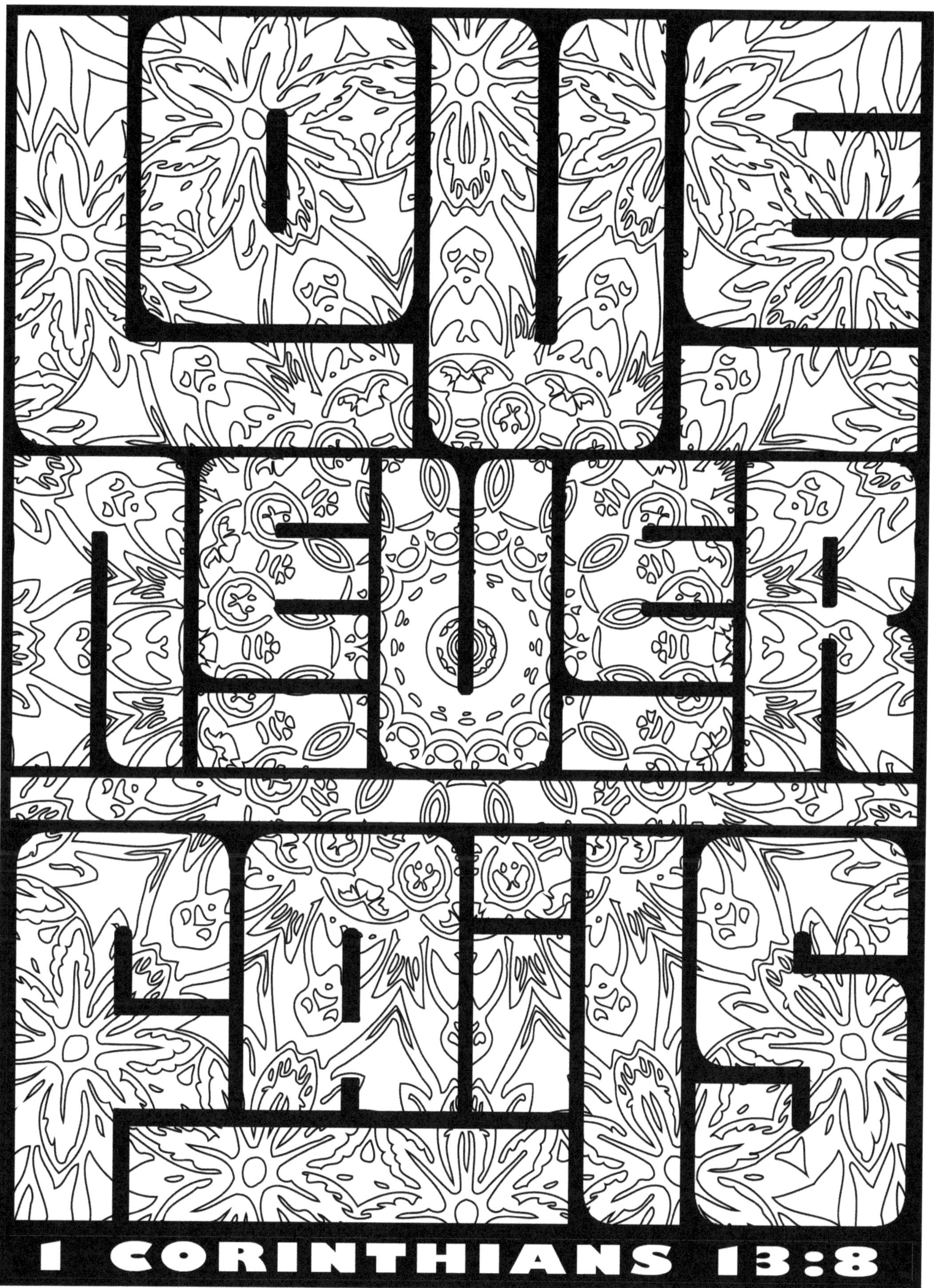
LOVE
NEVER
FAILS
1 CORINTHIANS 13:8

"Pure love... It knows that only one thing is needed to please God: to do even the smallest things out of great love — love, and always love. Pure love never errs. Its light is strangely plentiful. It will not do anything that might displease God. It is ingenious at doing what is more pleasing to God, and no one will equal it. It is happy when it can empty itself and burn like a pure offering. The more it gives of itself, the happier it is. But also, no one can sense dangers from afar as can love; it knows how to unmask and also knows with whom it has to deal."

Saint Faustina
From the *Diary of Saint Faustina,* #140
www.divinemercy.org

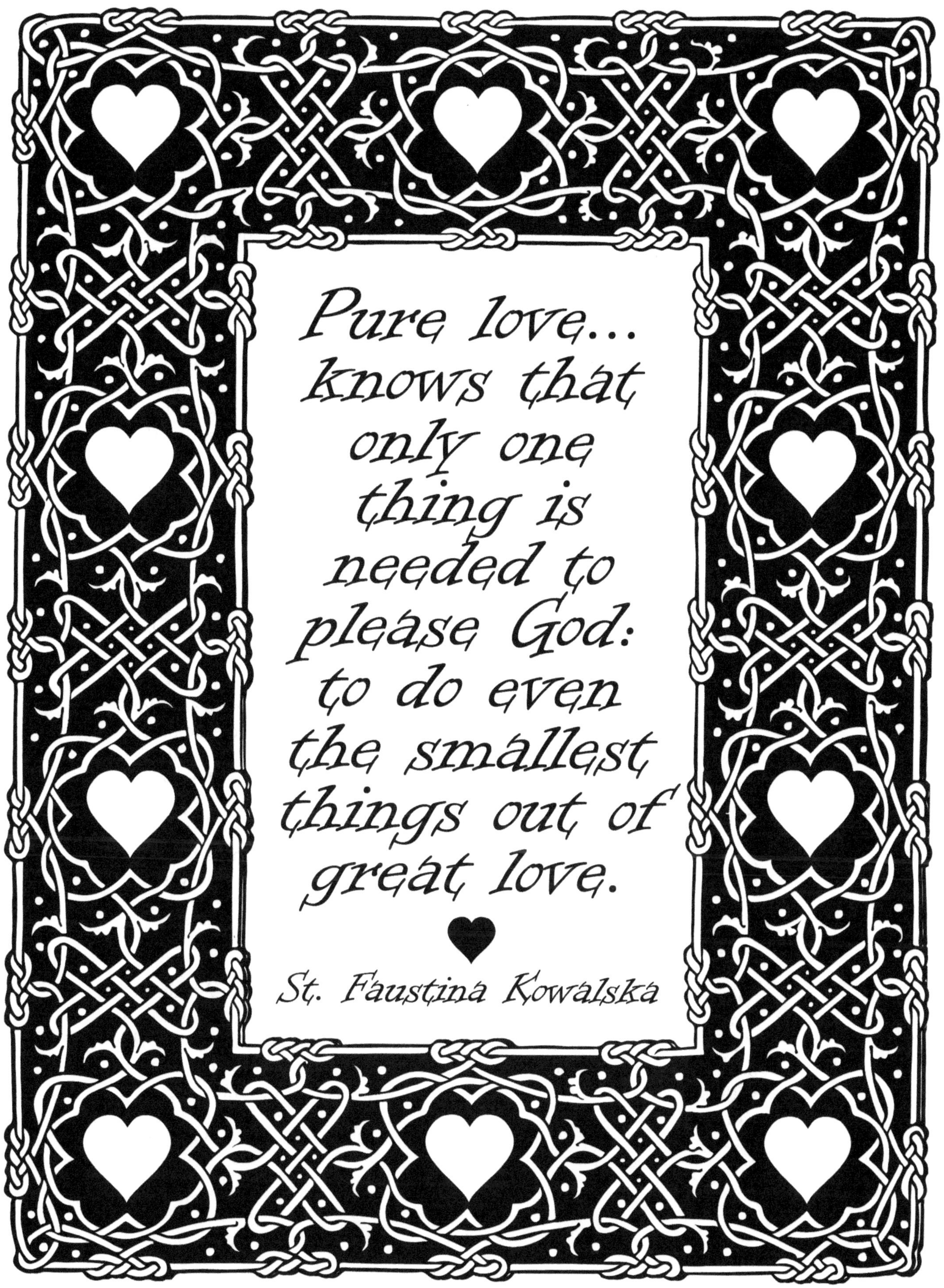
Pure love...
knows that
only one
thing is
needed to
please God:
to do even
the smallest
things out of
great love.
St. Faustina Kowalska

Some sayings of Saint Vincent de Paul regarding love:

"Our vocation is to go and enflame the heart of men, to do what the Son of God did, He who brought fire into the world to set it alight with His love. What else can we wish for, than for it to burn and consume all things?

"Thus it is true that I have been sent not only to love God, but also to make men love Him.

"It is not enough to love God if my neighbor does not love Him. I must love my neighbor as the image of God and the object of His love, and do everything so that in their turn men love their Creator who knows and considers them as His brothers, whom He has saved; I must obtain that they love each other with mutual love, out of love for God who loved them to the point of abandoning to death His very Son. So that is my duty. Now, if it is true that we are called to bear God's love near and far, if we must set nations alight, if our vocation is to go and spread this divine fire in the whole world, if it is so, my brothers, if it is really so, how must I myself burn of this divine fire!

"How can we give love to others, if we do not have it among us? Let us look if it is so, not generally, but if each one has it within himself, in due amount; because if love is not on fire in us, if we do not love each other as Jesus Christ loved us and if we do not act as he did, how can we hope to spread such love throughout the world? You cannot give what you do not have. The precise duty of charity consists in doing to others what you reasonably would like done to yourself. Do I really behave towards my neighbor as I wish he would towards me?"

Saint Vincent de Paul
From "Conferences to the Priests of the Mission"

Saint Vincent de Paul (1581–1660) was a French priest who dedicated himself to serving the poor. He became known as the "Great Apostle of Charity." Inspired by his great works of compassion and generosity, The Society of St. Vincent de Paul was founded in 1833 to help provide the poor with food and other necessities and is now in many parishes throughout the world.

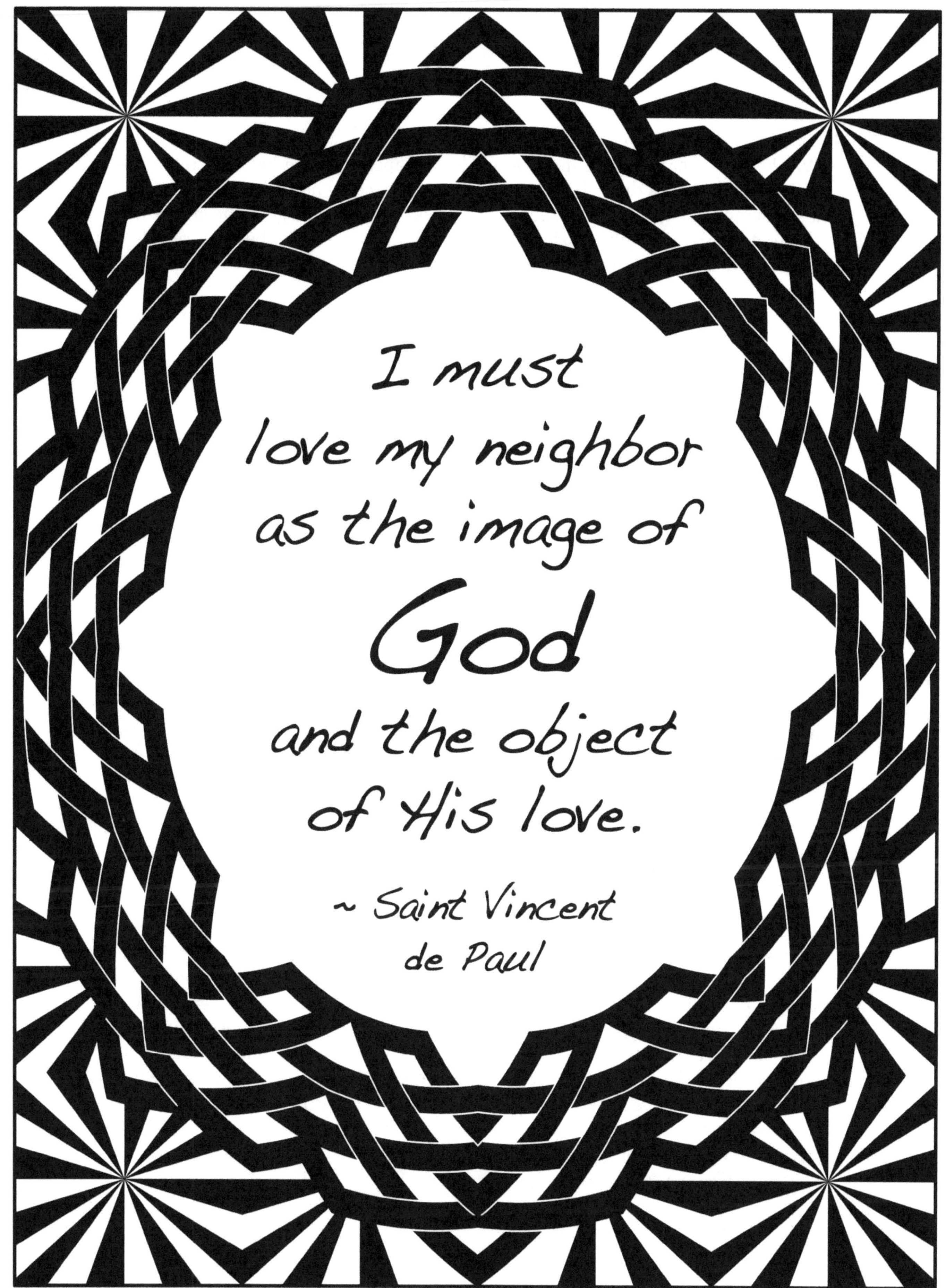
I must
love my neighbor
as the image of
God
and the object
of His love.
~ Saint Vincent
de Paul

"We become what we love and who we love shapes what we become. If we love things, we become a thing. If we love nothing, we become nothing. Imitation is not a literal mimicking of Christ, rather it means becoming the image of the beloved, an image disclosed through transformation. This means we are to become vessels of God's compassionate love for others."

Saint Clare of Assisi

Saint Clare of Assisi (1194–1253) is an Italian saint and one of the first followers of Saint Francis of Assisi. She cofounded the Order of Poor Ladies, or Clares, a monastic religious order for women in the Franciscan tradition, and wrote their Rule of Life, the first set of monastic guidelines known to have been written by a woman.

From her earliest years, Clare seems to have been endowed with the rarest virtues. As a child she was most devoted to prayer and to practices of mortification, and as she as time went by her distaste for the world and her yearning for a more spiritual life increased. She was eighteen years of age when St. Francis came to preach, and his words kindled a flame in her heart. She sought him out secretly and begged him to help her that she too might live "after the manner of the holy Gospel". St. Francis, who at once recognized in Clare one of those chosen souls destined by God for great things, promised to assist her. On Palm Sunday, Clare, arrayed in all her finery, attended high Mass at the cathedral, but when the others pressed forward to the altar-rail to receive a branch of palm, she remained in her place as if rapt in a dream. All eyes were upon the young girl as the bishop descended from the sanctuary and placed the palm in her hand. That was the last time the world beheld Clare. That night she secretly left her father's house by St. Francis's advice and, accompanied by her aunt Bianca and another companion, proceeded to the humble chapel of the Porziuncula, where St. Francis and his disciples met her with lights in their hands. Clare then laid aside her rich dress, and St. Francis, having cut off her hair, clothed her in a rough tunic and a thick veil. In this way, the young heroine vowed herself to the service of Jesus Christ. This was March 20, 1212. Clare was placed by St. Francis provisionally with the Benedictine nuns, but her father who was upset and furious tried to dissuade her and force her to come back home. But Clare held her own with a firmness above her years. Eventually she and her sister Agnes were established by St. Francis in a rude dwelling adjoining the poor chapel of San Damiano outside the town, which he had to a great extent rebuilt with his own hands, and which he now obtained from the Benedictines as a permanent abode for his spiritual daughters. Thus was founded the first community of the Order of Poor Ladies, or of Poor Clares, as this second order of St. Francis came to be called. (Adapted from *The Catholic Encyclopedia*, 1913 edition.)

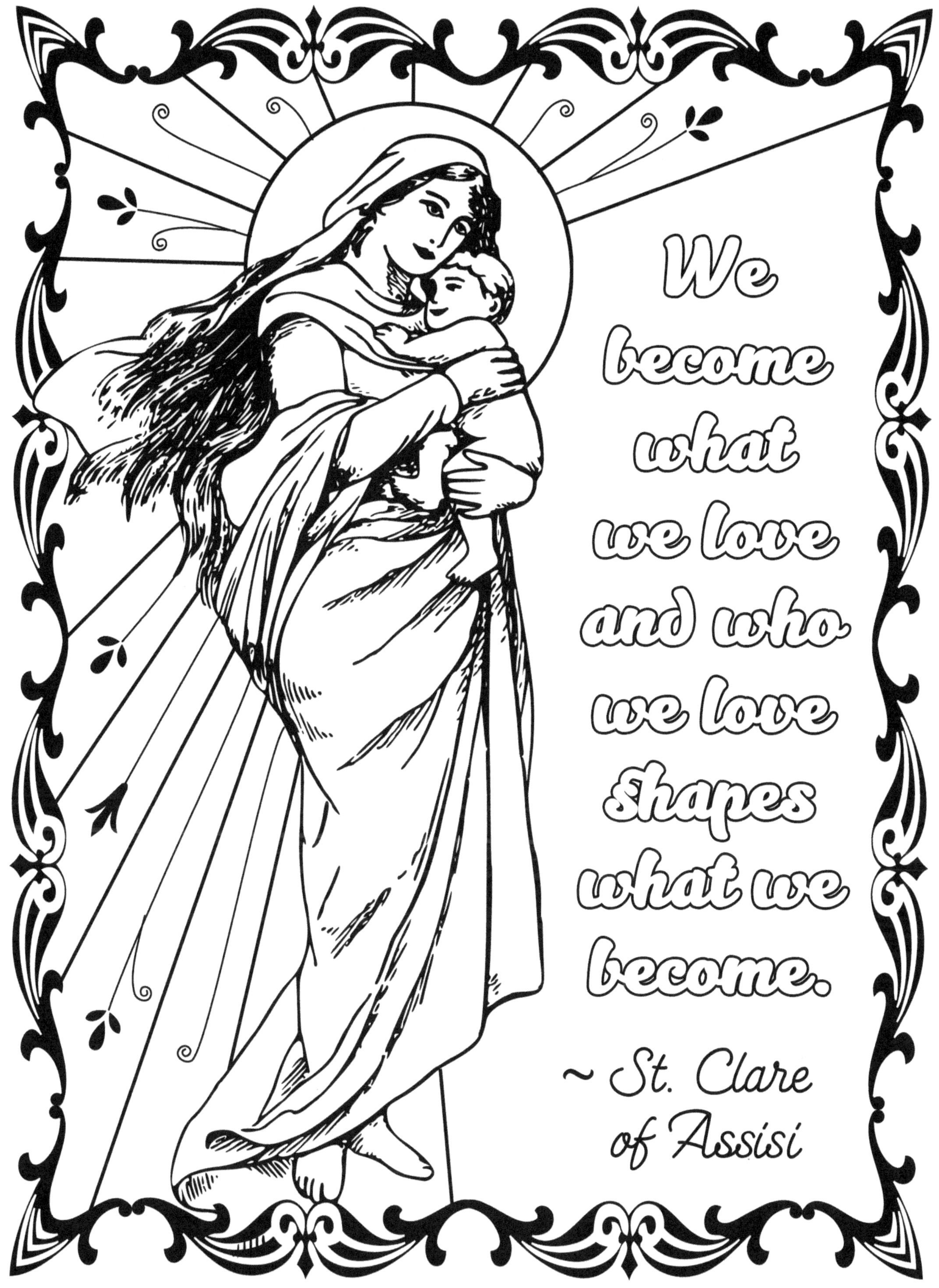
We
become
what
we love
and who
we love
shapes
what we
become.
~ St. Clare
of Assisi

"I will now describe, as I promised, the difference between sweetness in prayer and spiritual consolations.... In that of which I speak, the tears and good desires are often partly caused by the natural disposition, but although this may be the case, yet, as I said, these feelings terminate in God. Sensible devotion is very desirable if the soul is humble enough to understand that it is not more holy on account of these sentiments, which cannot always with certainty be ascribed to charity, and even then are still the gift of God.

"These feelings of devotion are most common with souls in the first three mansions, who are nearly always using their understanding and reason in making meditations. This is good for them, for they have not been given grace for more; they should, however, try occasionally to elicit some acts such as praising God, rejoicing in His goodness and that He is what He is: let them desire that He may be honored and glorified. They must do this as best they can, for it greatly inflames the will. Let them be very careful, when God gives these sentiments, not to set them aside in order to finish their accustomed meditation. But, having spoken fully on this subject elsewhere, [*Life*, chapter xii. 2-4.] I will say no more now. I only wish to warn you that to make rapid progress and to reach the mansions we wish to enter, it is not so essential to *think* much as to *love* much: therefore you must practice whatever most excites you to this. Perhaps we do not know what love is, nor does this greatly surprise me. Love does not consist in great sweetness of devotion, but in a fervent determination to strive to please God in all things, in avoiding, as far as possible, all that would offend Him, and in praying for the increase of the glory and honor of His Son and for the growth of the Catholic Church. These are the signs of love; do not imagine that it consists in never thinking of anything but God, and that if your thoughts wander a little all is lost."

Saint Teresa of Avila
Interior Castle,
The Fourth Mansion, Chapter 1

Saint Teresa of Ávila, religious name **Teresa of Jesus,** (1515–1582) was a Carmelite nun, mystic, and the first woman to be proclaimed a Doctor of the Church. She initiated a reform of the Carmelite order along with St. John of the Cross, which eventually led to the establishment of the Discalced Carmelites. She wrote about growth in the spiritual life and the various stages of prayer, including mental prayer and contemplative prayer. Her books include her autobiography *The Life of Teresa of Jesus*, *The Interior Castle*, and *The Way of Perfection.*

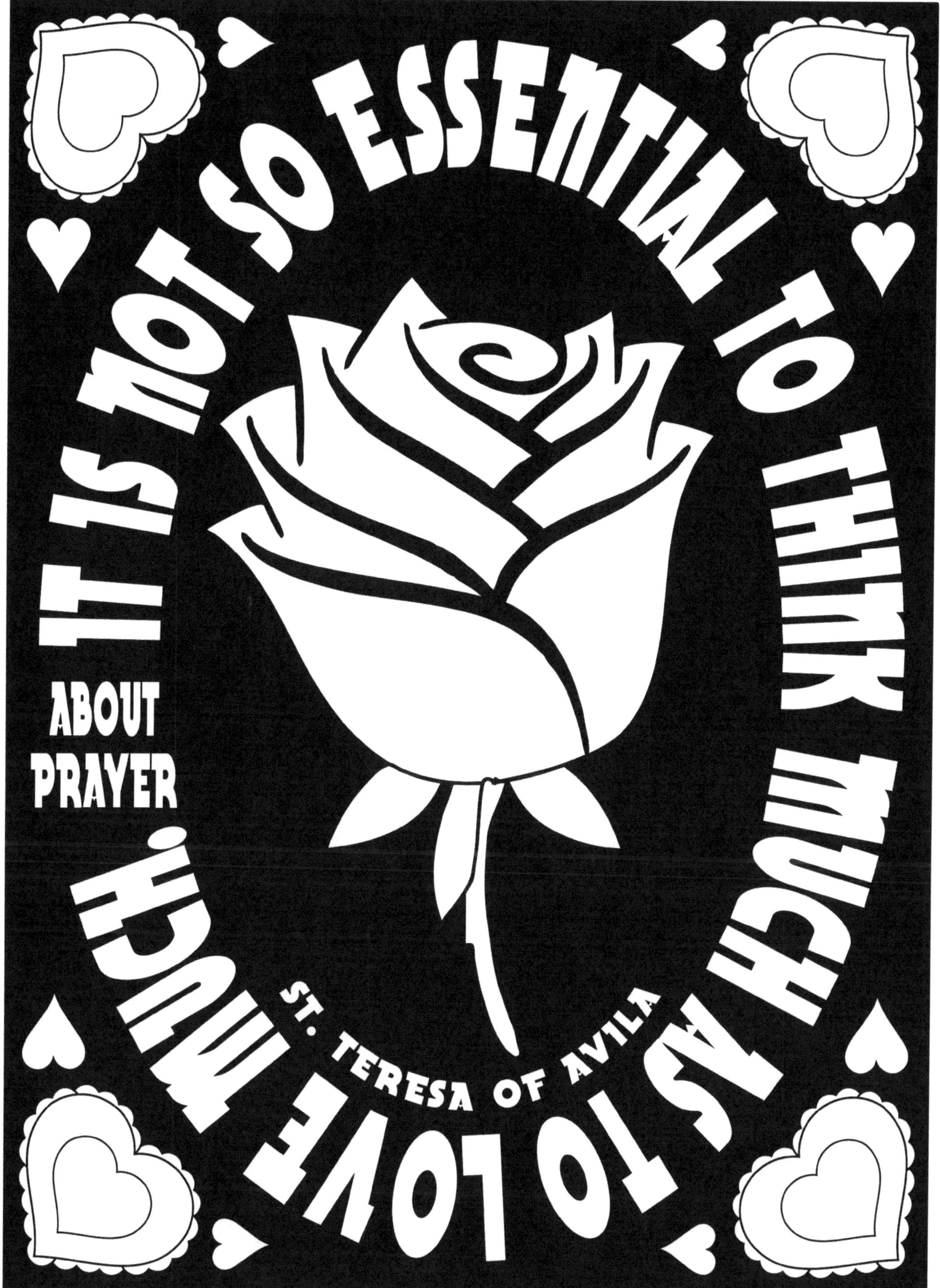
IT IS NOT SO ESSENTIAL TO THINK MUCH AS TO LOVE MUCH
ABOUT PRAYER
ST. TERESA OF AVILA

Some sayings of St. Teresa of Calcutta (Mother Teresa) regarding love:

“If you judge people, you have no time to love them.”

“There are no great things, only small things with great love.”

“Spread love everywhere you go. Let no one ever come to you without leaving happier.”

“I have found the paradox that if I love until it hurts, then there is no hurt, but only more love.”

“Let us always meet each other with smile, for the smile is the beginning of love.”

“Love is a fruit in season at all times, and within reach of every hand.”

“Love begins by taking care of the closest ones--the ones at home.”

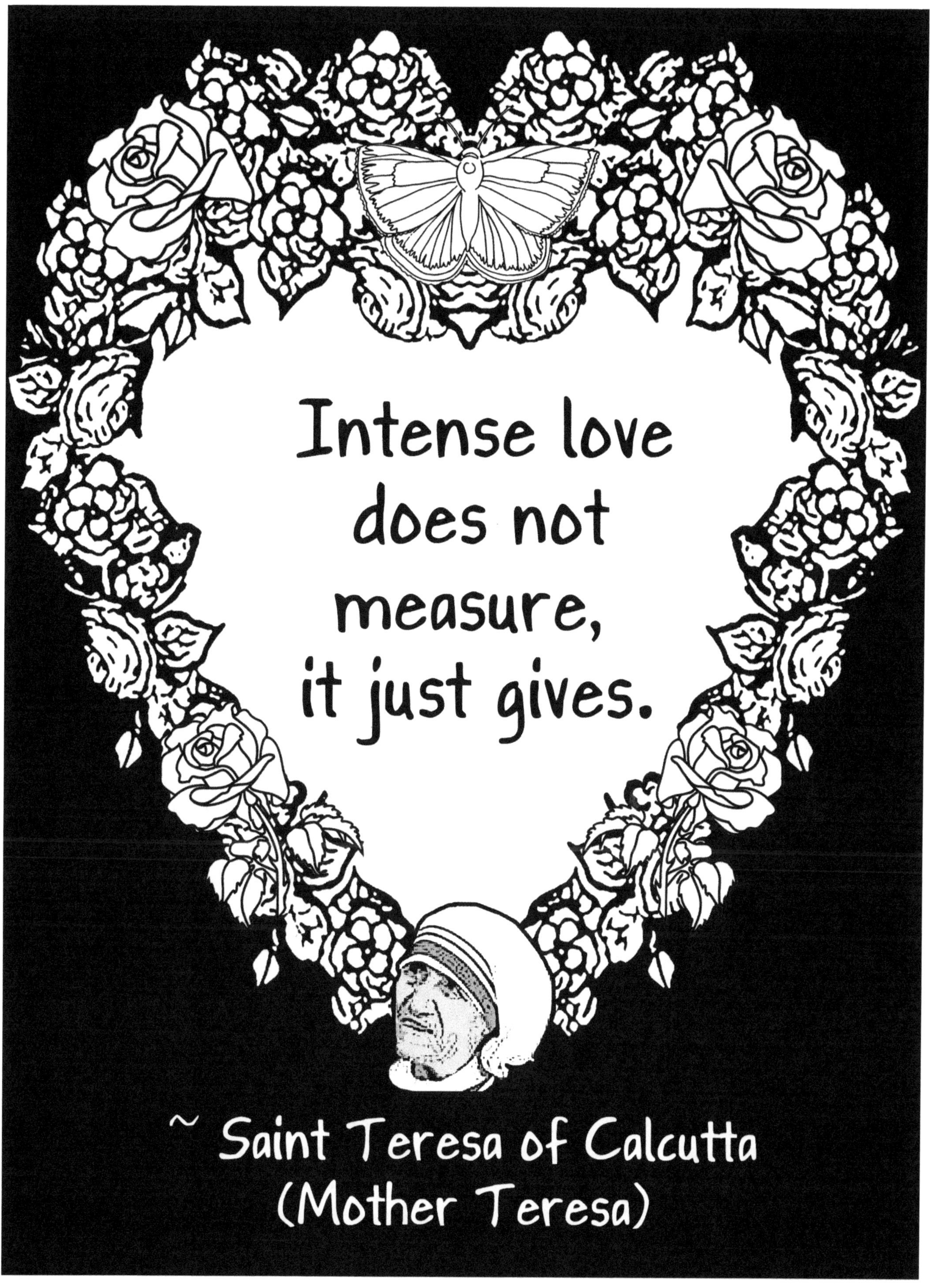
Intense love
does not
measure,
it just gives.
~ Saint Teresa of Calcutta
(Mother Teresa)

"And now coming back to the story of the young man in the Gospels, we see that he heard the call—'Follow me'—but that he 'went away sad, for he had many possessions.'

"The sadness of the young man makes us reflect. We could be tempted to think that many possessions, many of the goods of this world, can bring happiness. We see instead in the case of the young man in the Gospel that his many possessions had become an obstacle to accepting the call of Jesus to follow him. He was not ready to say *yes* to Jesus, and *no* to self, to say *yes* to love and *no*t to escape.

"Real love is demanding. I would fail in my mission if I did not clearly tell you so. For it was Jesus—our Jesus himself—who said: 'You are my friends if you do what I command you' (*John* 15:14). Love demands effort and a personal commitment to the will of God. It means discipline and sacrifice, but it also means joy and human fulfillment....

"And, as a last word to all of you who listen to me tonight, I would say this : the reason for my mission, for my journey, through the United States is to tell you, to tell everyone—young and old alike—to say to everyone in the name of Christ: 'Come and follow me !' "

Pope Saint John Paul II
From his homily at Holy Mass on Boston Common,
Monday, October 1, 1979

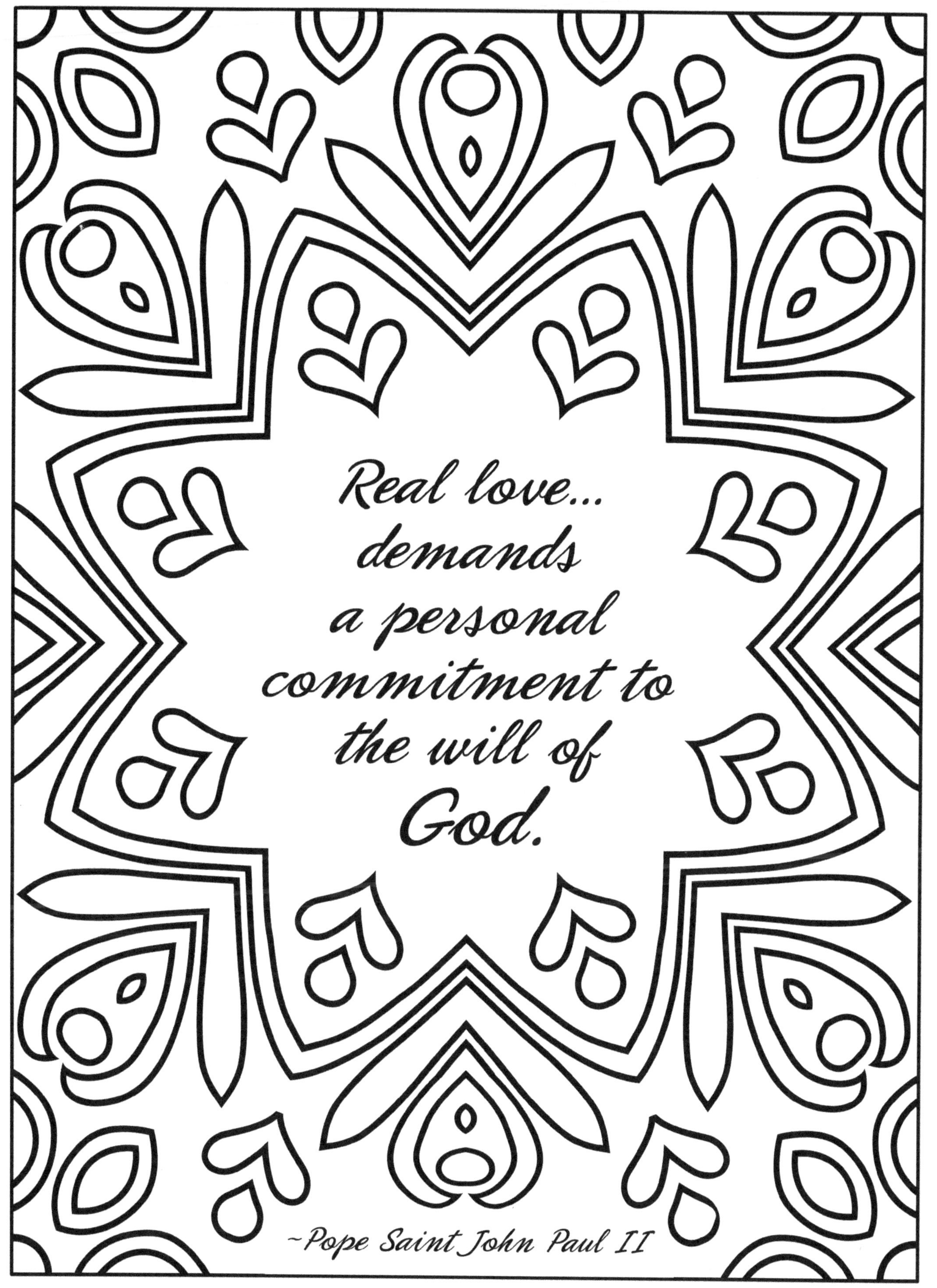
Real love...
demands
a personal
commitment to
the will of
God.
~Pope Saint John Paul II

"Too late I loved you, O Beauty ever ancient and ever new! Too late I loved you! And, behold, you were within me, and I out of myself, and there I searched for you."

Saint Augustine of Hippo
Introduction to a Philosophy of Religion (1970)
by Alice Von Hildebrand

Some other sayings of Saint Augustine of Hippo regarding love:

"Find out how much God has given you and from it take what you need; the remainder is needed by others."

"Thou hast created us for thyself, and our heart is not quiet until it rests in Thee."

"Love, and do what you like."

"How is the Father's love for us proved? By the fact that he sent his only Son to die for us. As the apostle Paul says, 'He who did not spare his own Son, but delivered him up for us all, how will he not freely give us all things?' [Rom. 8:32] Notice how the Father delivered up Christ, and so did Judas. Does it not seem that they did the same sort of thing? . . . There was a delivering up by the Father; a delivering up [of himself] by the Son, and a delivering up by Judas. The thing done is the same, but what is it that sets their actions apart? This: the Father and the Son did it in love, but Judas did it in betrayal. So you see that we need to consider not what a person does but with what mind and will he does it. Why do we bless the Father and detest Judas for doing the same deed? We bless love and detest wickedness. What I have said so far applies to actions that are similar. When they are different, we find people made fierce by love; and by wickedness made seductively gentle. A father beats a boy, while a kidnapper caresses him. Offered a choice between blows and caresses, who would not choose the caresses and avoid the blows? But when you consider the people who give them you realize that it is love that beats, wickedness that caresses. This is what I insist upon: human actions can only be understood by their root in love. All kinds of actions might appear good without proceeding from the root of love. Remember, thorns also have flowers: some actions seem truly savage, but are done for the sake of discipline motivated by love. Once and for all, I give you this one short command: love, and do what you will. If you hold your peace, hold your peace out of love. If you cry out, cry out in love. If you correct someone, correct them out of love. If you spare them, spare them out of love. Let the root of love be in you: nothing can spring from it but good."

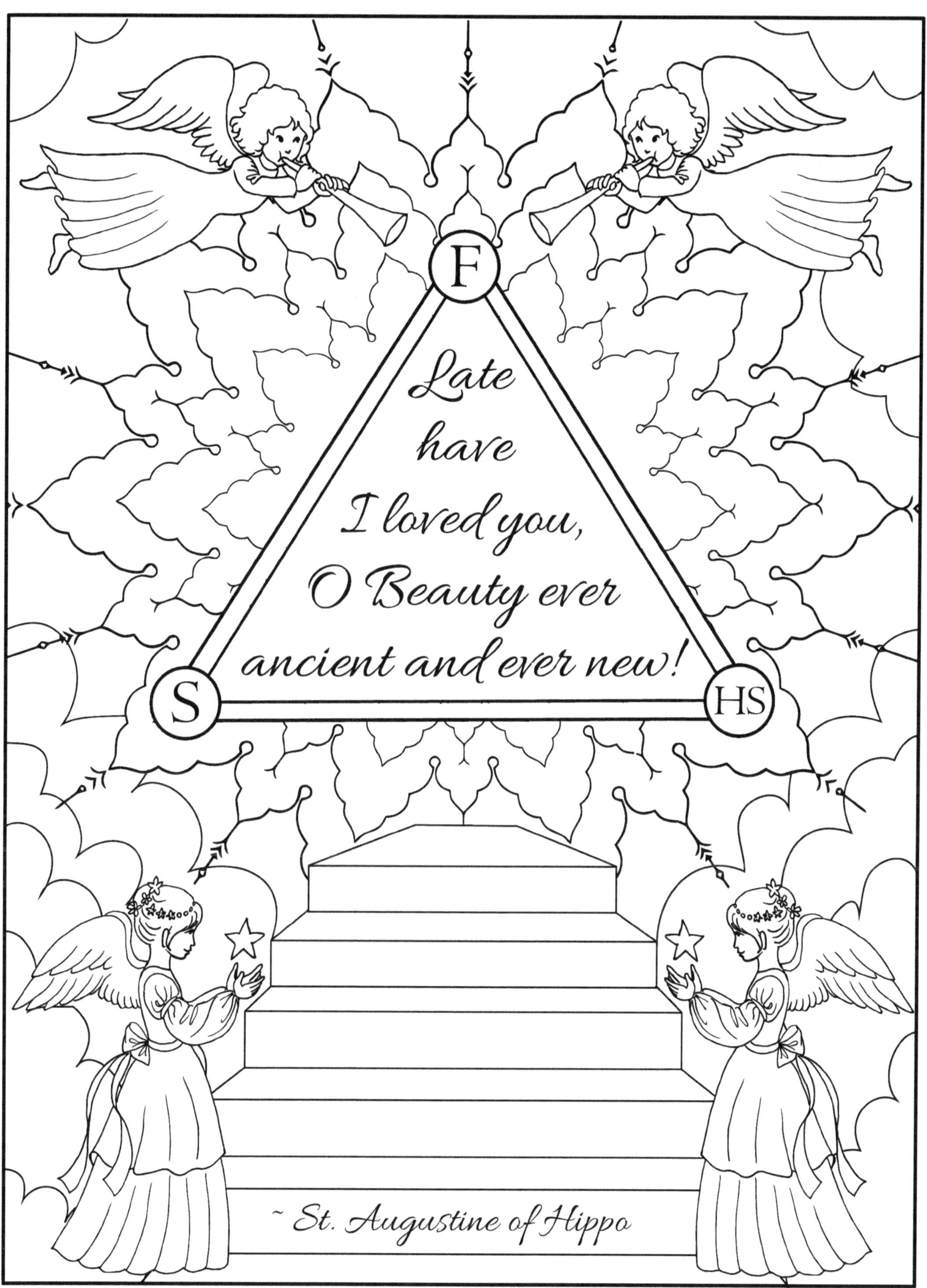
F
S
HS
Late
have
I loved you,
O Beauty ever
ancient and ever new!
~ St. Augustine of Hippo

"The Eucharist is the Sacrament of Love. It signifies Love. It produces love. The Eucharist is the consummation of the whole spiritual life."

Saint Thomas Aquinas

Saint Thomas Aquinas (1225–1274) was a Dominican friar, priest, writer, and Doctor of the Church from Italy. He had a great influence on modern philosophy using both natural reason and theology. His best known writings are the *Summa Theologica* and the *Summa contra Gentiles*. He also wrote Eucharistic hymns. His works are still part of priestly formation, and he is considered one of the Church's greatest theologians and philosophers.

St. Thomas's life may be summed up in a few words: praying, preaching, teaching, writing, journeying. Popes and others wished to hear him. He was always teaching and writing, living on earth with one passion, an ardent zeal for the explanation and defense of Christian truth. So devoted was he to his sacred task that with tears he begged to be excused from accepting the Archbishopric of Naples, to which he was appointed by Clement IV. Had this appointment been accepted, most probably the *Summa Theologica* would not have been written. During prayer, he was frequently in ecstasy, and this became more frequent towards the end of his life. On one occasion after he had completed his treatise on the Eucharist, three of the brethren saw him lifted in ecstasy, and they heard a voice proceeding from the crucifix on the altar, saying, "Thou hast written well of me, Thomas; what reward wilt thou have?" Thomas said, "None other than Thyself, Lord." (Prümmer, op. cit., p. 38). In 1273, he laid aside his pen and would write no more. That day he experienced an unusually long ecstasy during Mass; what was revealed to him we can only surmise from his reply to Father Reginald, who urged him to continue his writings: "I can do no more. Such secrets have been revealed to me that all I have written now appears to be of little value" (*modica*, Prümmer, op. cit., p. 43). The *Summa Theologica* had been completed only as far as the ninetieth question of the third part. When he was nearing death and the Sacred Viaticum (Holy Communion) was brought into the room, he pronounced the following act of faith: "If in this world there be any knowledge of this sacrament stronger than that of faith, I wish now to use it in affirming that I firmly believe and know as certain that Jesus Christ, True God and True Man, Son of God and Son of the Virgin Mary, is in this Sacrament . . . I receive Thee, the price of my redemption, for Whose love I have watched, studied, and labored. Thee have I preached; Thee have I taught. Never have I said anything against Thee: if anything was not well said, that is to be attributed to my ignorance. Neither do I wish to be obstinate in my opinions, but if I have written anything erroneous concerning this sacrament or other matters, I submit all to the judgment and correction of the Holy Roman Church, in whose obedience I now pass from this life." He died on March 7, 1274. Numerous miracles attested his sanctity, and he was canonized by John XXII, July 18, 1323. (Adapted from *The Catholic Encyclopedia*, 1913 edition.)

⇨

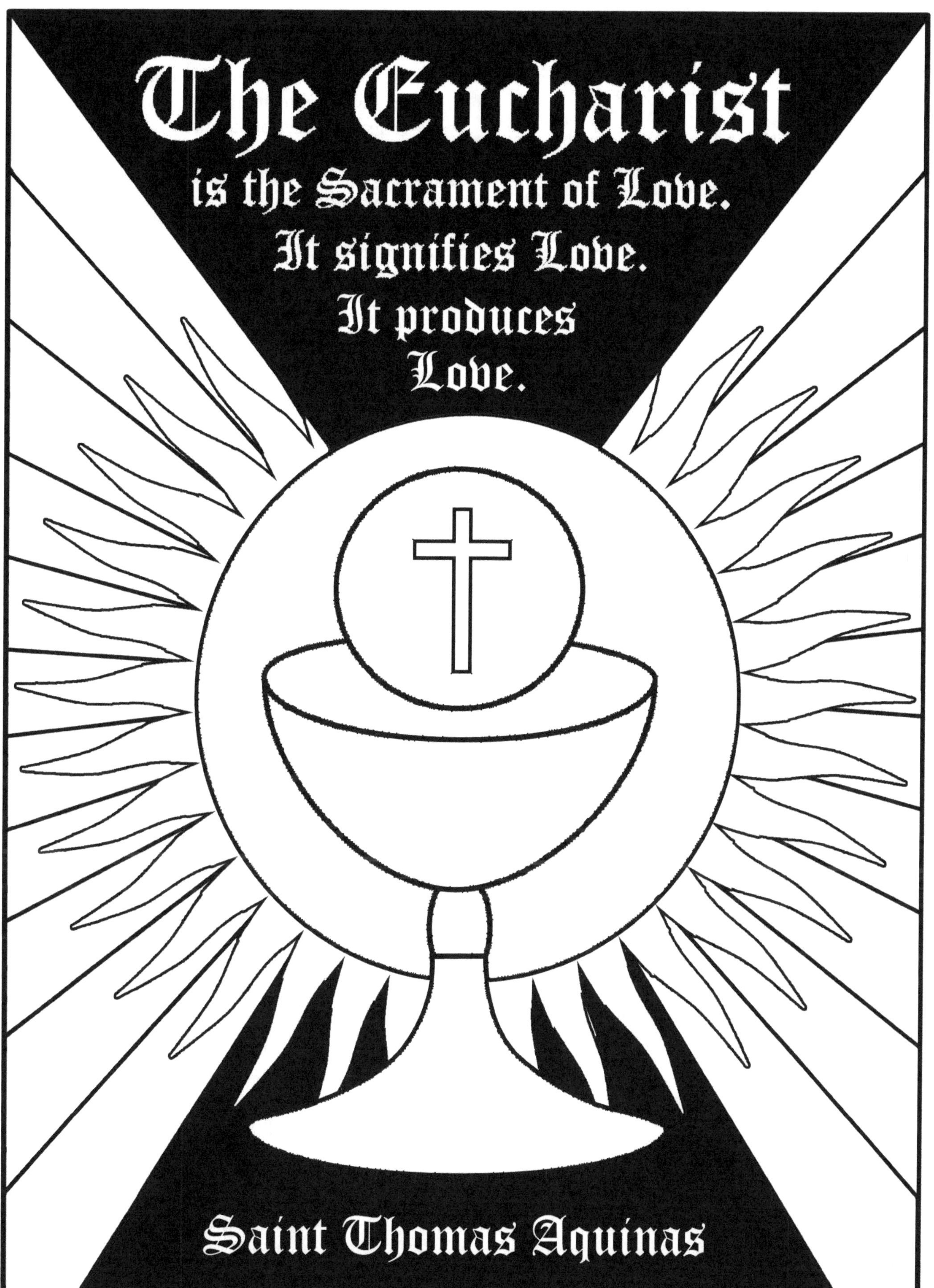
The Eucharist
is the Sacrament of Love.
It signifies Love.
It produces
Love.
Saint Thomas Aquinas

Saint Benedict of Nursia
(480 – 543 or 547)
From *The Rule of Saint Benedict,* Chapter 4:

The instruments of good works:

1. First of all, to love the Lord thy God with all thy heart, with all thy soul, and with all thy strength.
2. Then, to love thy neighbor as thyself.
3. Next, not to kill.
4. Not to commit adultery.
5. Not to steal.
6. Not to covet.
7. Not to bear false witness.
8. To honor all men.
9. Not to do to another what one would not have done to oneself.
10. To deny oneself in order to follow Christ
11. To chastise the body.
12. Not to seek after luxuries.
13. To love fasting.
14. To refresh the poor.
15. To clothe the naked.
16. To visit the sick.
17. To bury the dead.
18. To help in affliction.
19. To console the sorrowing.
20. To keep aloof from worldly actions.
21. To prefer nothing to the love of Christ.
22. Not to follow the promptings of anger.
23. Not to seek an occasion of revenge.
24. Not to foster deceit in one's heart.
25. Not to make a feigned peace.
26. Not to forsake charity.
27. Not to swear, lest perhaps one perjure oneself.
28. To utter the truth with heart and lips.
29. Not to render evil for evil.
30. To do no wrong to anyone, but to bear patiently any wrong done to oneself.
31. To love one's enemies.
32. Not to speak ill of those who speak ill of us, but rather to speak well of them.
33. To suffer persecution for justice' sake.
34. Not to be proud.
35. Not to be given to wine.
36. Not to be a glutton.
37. Not to be given to sleep.
38. Not to be slothful.
39. Not to be a murmurer.
40. Not to be a detractor.
41. To put one's trust in God.
42. To attribute any good one sees in oneself to God and not to oneself.
43. But always to acknowledge that the evil is one's own, and to attribute it to oneself.
44. To fear the days of judgment.
45. To be in dread of hell.
46. To desire everlasting life with all spiritual longing.
47. To keep death daily before one's eyes.
48. To keep guard at all times over the actions of one's life.
49. To know for certain that God sees one in every place.
50. To dash upon Christ one's evil thoughts the instant they come to one's heart, and to manifest them to one's spiritual father.
51. To keep one's mouth from speech that is wicked or full of guile.
52. Not to love much speaking.
53. Not to speak words that are vain or such as provoke laughter.
54. Not to love much or noisy laughter.
55. To listen willingly to holy reading.
56. To apply oneself frequently to prayer.
57. Daily with tears and sighs to confess one's sins to God in prayer, and to amend these evils for the future.
58. Not to fulfill the desires of the flesh.
59. To hate one's own will.
60. To obey in all things the commands of the Abbot, even though he himself (which God forbid) should act otherwise, being mindful of that precept of the Lord: "What they say, do ye; but what they do, do ye not"
61. Not to wish to be called holy before one is so, but first to be holy that one may be truly so called.
62. To fulfill the commandments of God daily by one's deeds.
63. To love chastity.
64. To hate no man.
65. To have no jealousy or envy.
66. Not to love strife.
67. To fly from vainglory.
68. To reverence one's seniors.
69. To love one's juniors.
70. To pray for one's enemies in the love of Christ
71. To make peace with those with whom one is at variance before the setting of the sun.
72. And never to despair of God's mercy.

⇨

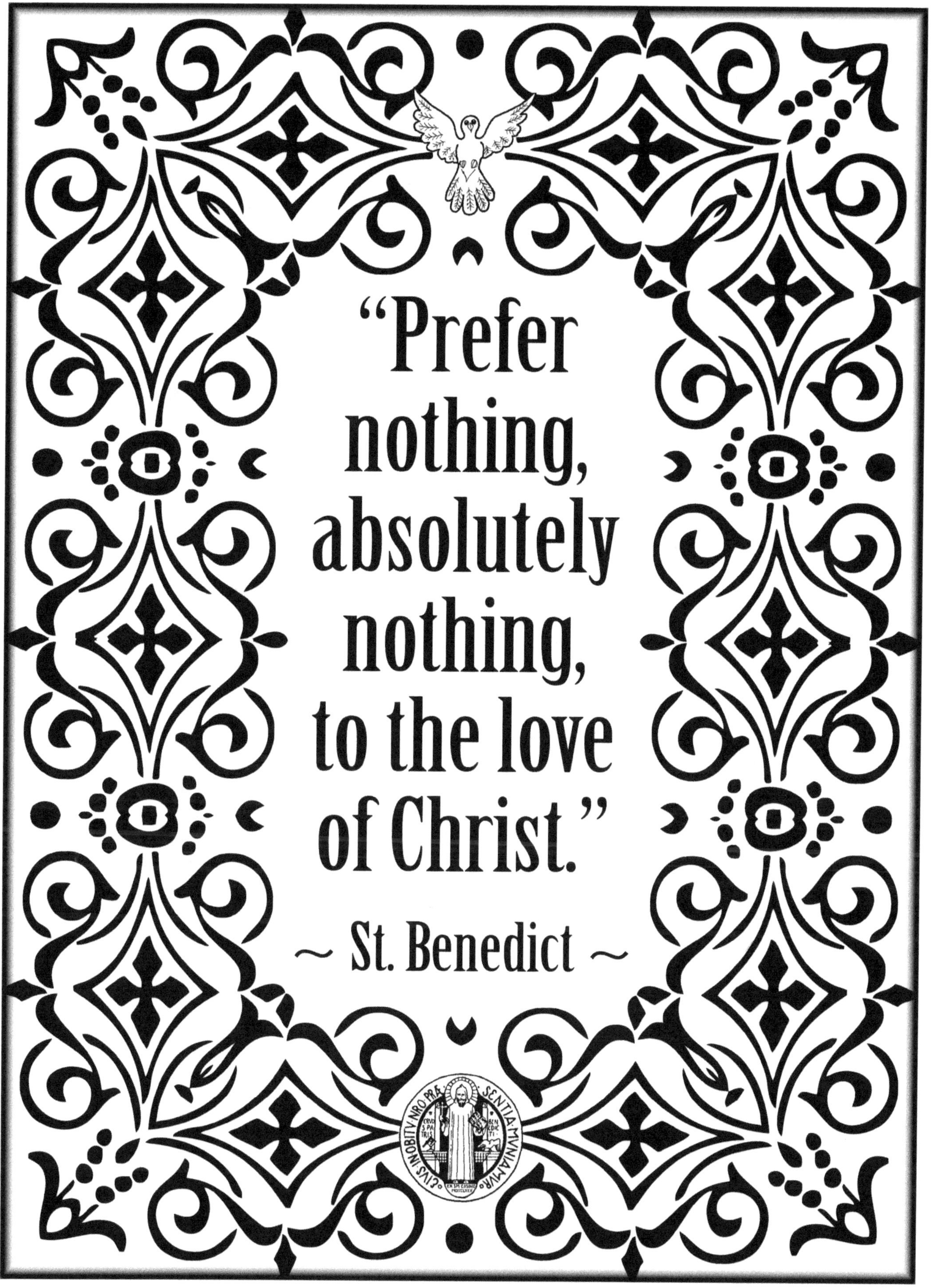
"Prefer
nothing,
absolutely
nothing,
to the love
of Christ."
~ St. Benedict ~

"Do not accept anything as the truth if it lacks love, and do not accept anything as love which lacks truth! One without the other becomes a destructive lie."

St Teresa Benedicta of the Cross

Edith Stein, religious name **Teresa Benedicta of the Cross** (1891–1942), was born into an observant Jewish family in Germany. She ended up being an atheist in her teens. She obtained a doctorate of philosophy from the University of Freiburg and became a member of the faculty there where she worked as a teaching assistant. Eventually after reading St. Teresa of Avila's autobiography, she recognized it as "the truth", converted to Catholicism, and became a Discalced Carmelite nun.

In 1938, she and her sister Rosa, who was a convert and an extern sister (a member of the Carmelite community who took care of the community's needs outside the monastery), were sent to the Carmelite monastery in Echt, Netherlands in an effort to protect them from the Nazi persecution of the Jews. However, a few years after the Nazis invaded the Netherlands, they were arrested by them on August 2, 1942 because of their Jewish ancestry and were sent to the Auschwitz concentration camp, where they died in the gas chamber on August 9, 1942.

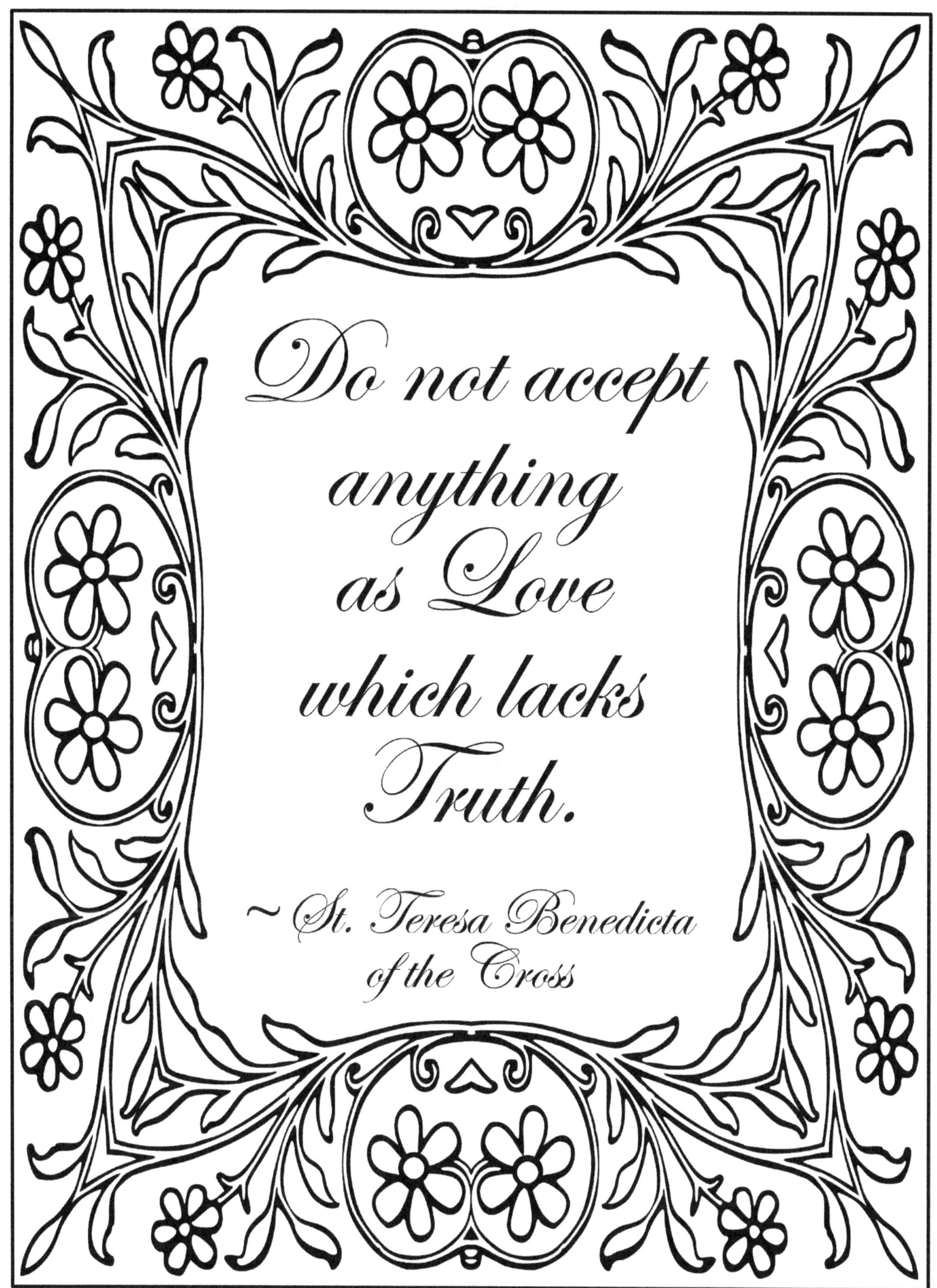
Do not accept
anything
as Love
which lacks
Truth.
~ St. Teresa Benedicta
of the Cross

"The proof of love is in the works. Where love exists, it works great things. But when it ceases to act, it ceases to exist."

Pope Saint Gregory the Great

Pope Saint Gregory I (540–604), commonly known as **Saint Gregory the Great**, is a Doctor of the Church and one of the Latin Fathers. He instigated the first known large-scale mission from Rome to convert pagans to Christianity. As pope, Gregory also wrote more than any previous pope. Gregory had a monastic background but also had political experience and was a great administrator. He did more for the welfare of the people in Rome than the emperors.

"Gregory is certainly one of the most notable figures in Ecclesiastical History. He has exercised in many respects a momentous influence on the doctrine, the organization, and the discipline of the Catholic Church. To him we must look for an explanation of the religious situation of the Middle Ages; indeed, if no account were taken of his work, the evolution of the form of medieval Christianity would be almost inexplicable. And further, in so far as the modern Catholic system is a legitimate development of medieval Catholicism, of this too Gregory may not unreasonably be termed the Father. Almost all the leading principles of the later Catholicism are found, at any rate in germ, in Gregory the Great." (F.H. Dudden, "Gregory the Great", 1, p. v).

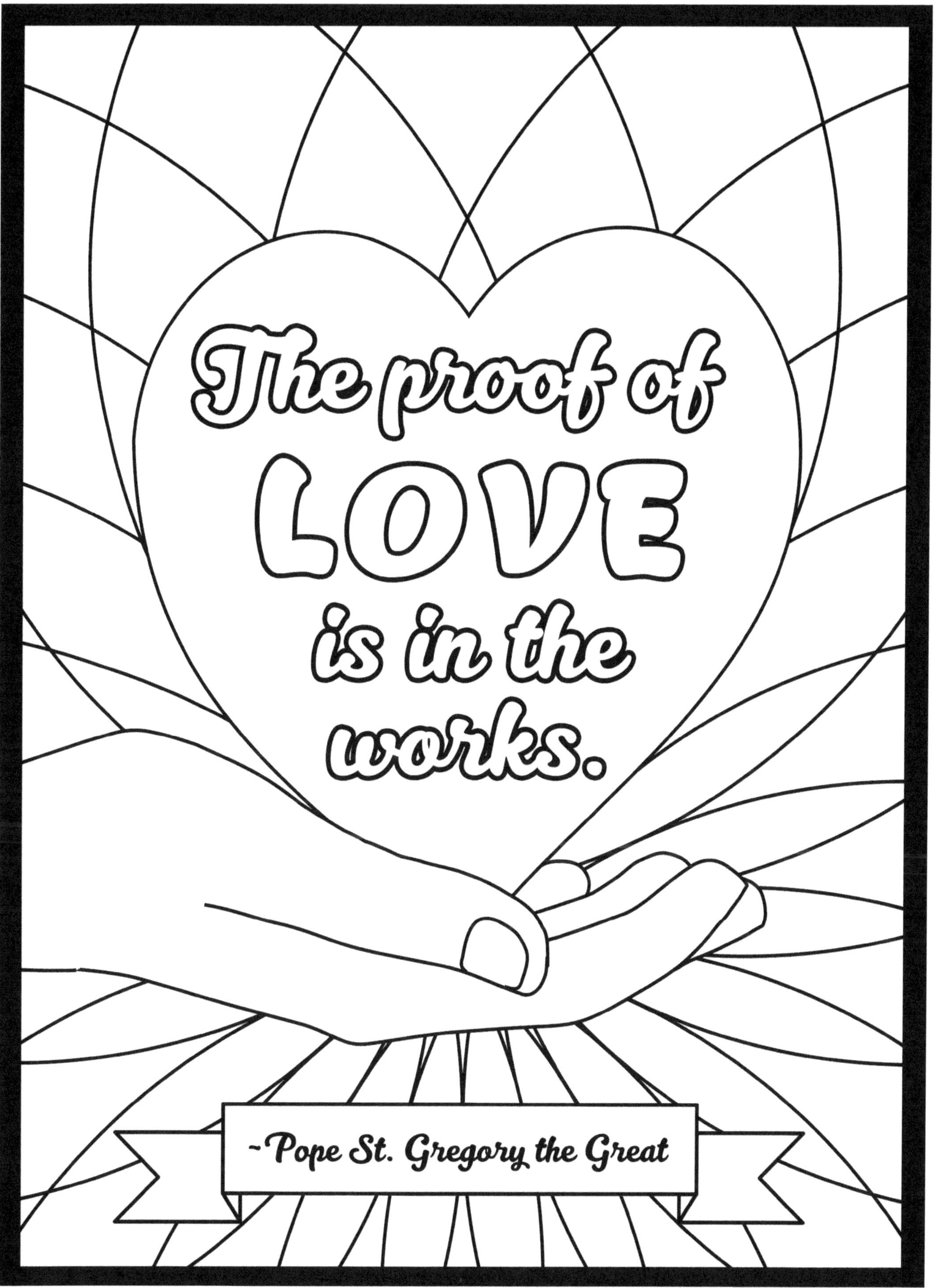
The proof of
LOVE
is in the
works.
~Pope St. Gregory the Great

Some sayings of Saint Teresa Benedicta of the Cross (Edith Stein):

"As for what concerns our relations with our fellow men, the anguish in our neighbor's soul must break all precept. All that we do is a means to an end, but love is an end in itself, because God is love."

"On the question of relating to our fellowman - our neighbor's spiritual need transcends every commandment. Everything else we do is a means to an end. But love is an end already, since God is love."

"One could say that in case of need, every normal and healthy woman is able to hold a position. And there is no profession which cannot be practiced by a woman."

"The limitless loving devotion to God, and the gift God makes of Himself to you, are the highest elevation of which the heart is capable; it is the highest degree of prayer. The souls that have reached this point are truly the heart of the Church."

"Things were in God's plan which I had not planned at all. I am coming to the living faith and conviction that - from God's point of view - there is no chance, and that the whole of my life, down to every detail, has been mapped out in God's divine providence and makes complete and perfect sense in God's all-seeing eyes."

"Those who join the Carmelite Order are not lost to their near and dear ones, but have been won for them, because it is our vocation to intercede to God for everyone."

Love is an end in itself, because God is love.

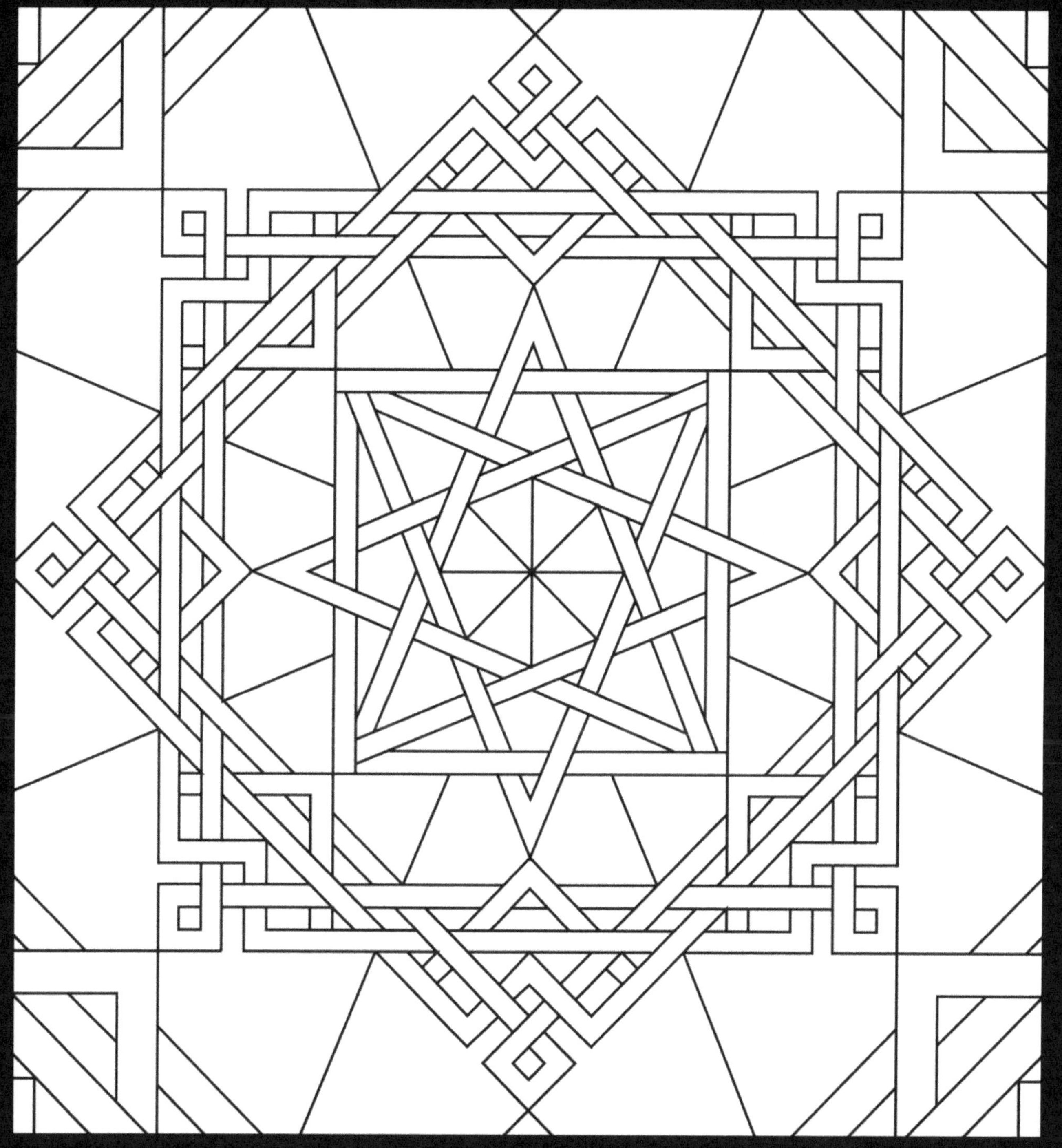

St. Teresa Benedicta of the Cross, OCD

"However, no one should judge that he has greater perfection, because he performs great penances, and gives himself in excess to the slaying of his body, than he who does less, inasmuch as neither virtue nor merit consists therein; for otherwise he would be in an evil case, who, from some legitimate reason, was unable to do actual penance. Merit consists in the virtue of love alone, flavored with the light of true discretion, without which the soul is worth nothing. And this love should be directed to Me endlessly, boundlessly, since I am the Supreme and Eternal Truth.... So you see how discreetly every soul, who wishes for grace, should pay her debts, that is, should love Me with an infinite love and without measure, but her neighbor with measure, with a restricted love, as I have said, not doing herself the injury of sin in order to be useful to others. This is Saint Paul's counsel to you when he says that charity ought to be concerned first with self, otherwise it will never be of perfect utility to others."

Saint Catherine of Siena
From *Dialog of Catherine of Siena*,
A Treatise of Discretion

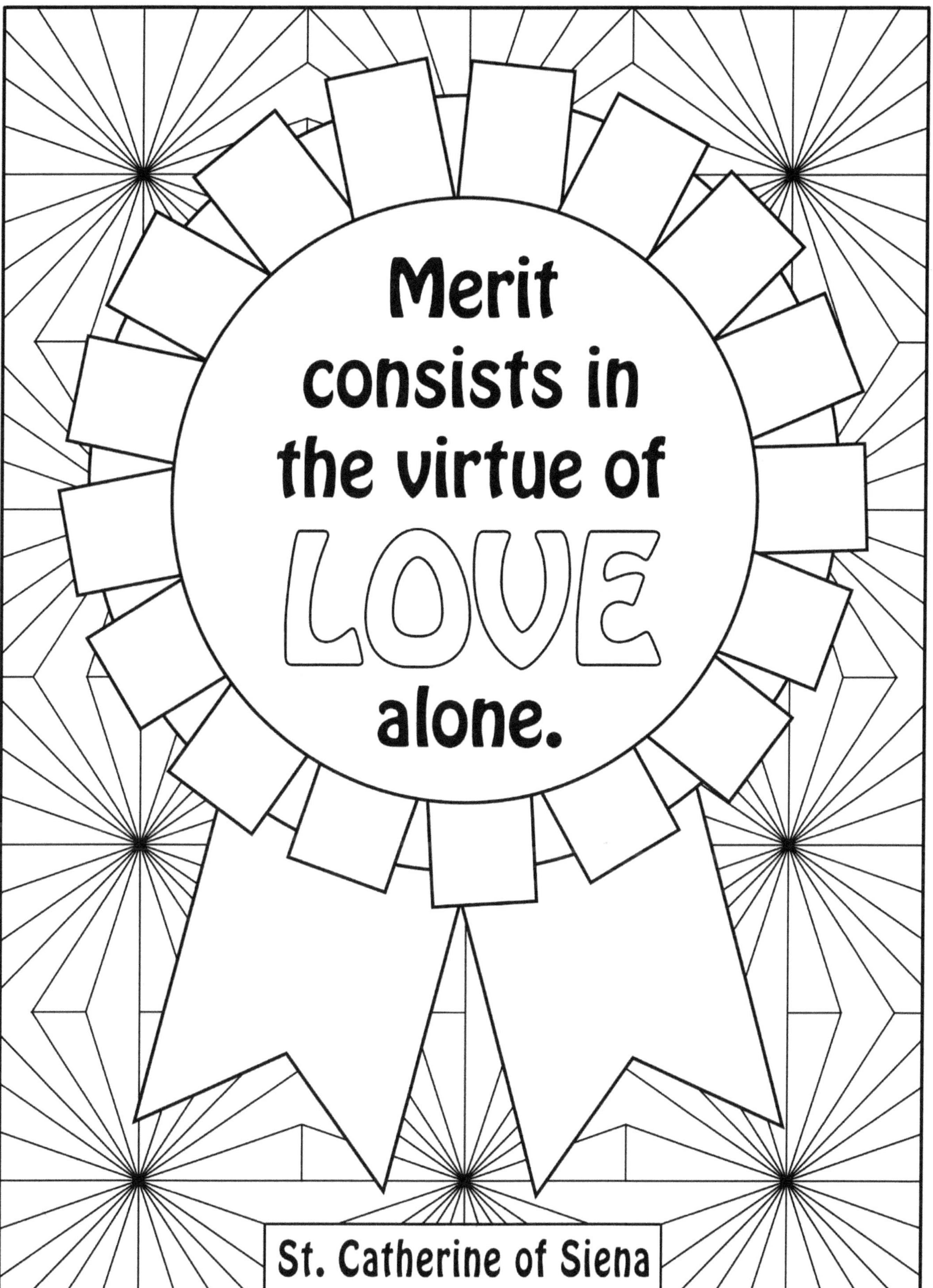
Merit
consists in
the virtue of
LOVE
alone.
St. Catherine of Siena

"What is the mark of love for your neighbor? Not to seek what is for your own benefit, but what is for the benefit of the one loved, both in body and in soul."

Saint Basil the Great

Saint Basil the Great (329 or 330–379) was a Greek bishop in Asia Minor (modern-day Turkey) and a Doctor of the Church. He was an influential theologian who fought against heresies such as Arianism. He befriended and cared for the poor. St. Basil is considered the father of monasticism in the Eastern Christianity similar to St. Benedict in the West as he established guidelines for monastic life.

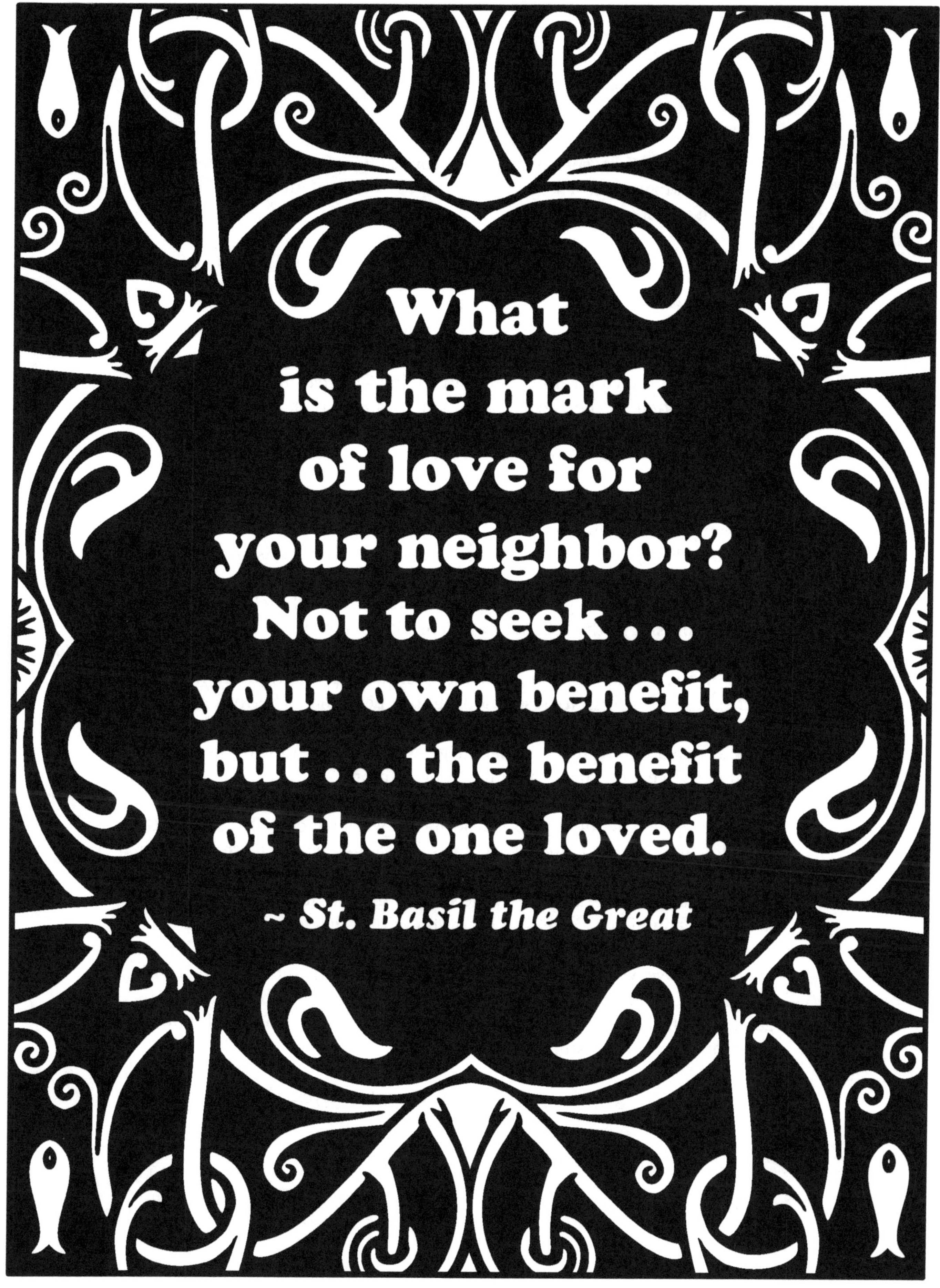
What
is the mark
of love for
your neighbor?
Not to seek . . .
your own benefit,
but . . . the benefit
of the one loved.
~ St. Basil the Great

"You learn to speak by speaking, to study by studying, to run by running, to work by working; and just so, you learn to love by loving. All those who think to learn in any other way deceive themselves."

Saint Francis de Sales

Francis de Sales (1567–1622) was a Bishop of Geneva and a Doctor of the Church. He is known for his writings including *Treatise on the Love of God* and *Introduction to the Devout Life,* which taught that all are called to spiritual perfection and holiness, not only religious but also lay people living in and involved in the affairs of the world.

"An *Introduction to the Devout Life*, a work intended to lead 'Philothea', the soul living in the world, into the paths of devotion, that is to say, of true and solid piety. Everyone should strive to become pious, and 'it is an error, it is even a heresy', to hold that piety is incompatible with any state of life. In the first part the author helps the soul to free itself from all inclination to, or affection for, sin; in the second, he teaches it how to be united to God by prayer and the sacraments; in the third, he exercises it in the practice of virtue; in the fourth, he strengthens it against temptation; in the fifth, he teaches it how to form its resolutions and to persevere. The Introduction, which is a masterpiece of psychology, practical morality, and common sense, was translated into nearly every language even in the lifetime of the author, and it has since gone through innumerable editions."

"*Treatise on the Love of God*, an authoritative work which reflects perfectly the mind and heart of Francis de Sales as a great genius and a great saint. It contains twelve books. The first four give us a history, or rather explain the theory, of Divine love, its birth in the soul, its growth, its perfection, and its decay and annihilation; the fifth book shows that this love is twofold - the love of complacency and the love of benevolence; the sixth and seventh treat of *affective* love, which is practiced in prayer; the eighth and ninth deal with *effective* love, that is, conformity to the will of God, and submission to His good pleasure. The last three resume what has preceded and teach how to apply practically the lessons taught therein."

Quoted paragraphs above from *The Catholic Encyclopedia,* 1913 edition

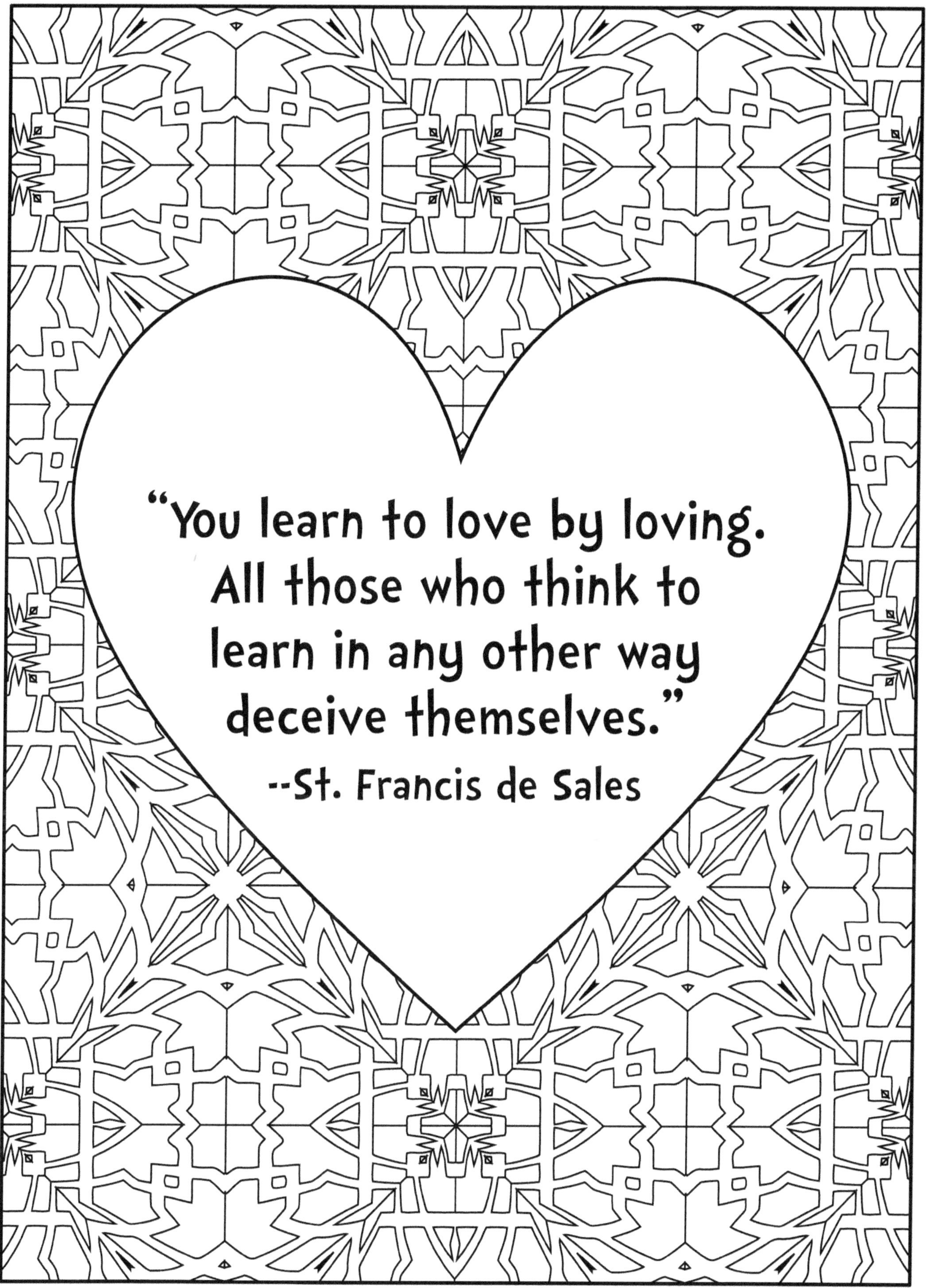
"You learn to love by loving.
All those who think to
learn in any other way
deceive themselves."
--St. Francis de Sales

CONTEMPLATION TO GAIN LOVE

"**Note**. First, it is well to remark two things: the first is that love ought to be put more in deeds than in words. The second, love consists in interchange between the two parties; that is to say in the lover's giving and communicating to the beloved what he has or out of what he has or can; and so, on the contrary, the beloved to the lover. So that if the one has knowledge, he give to the one who has it not. The same of honors, of riches; and so the one to the other.

"**Prayer**. The usual Prayer.
First Prelude. The first Prelude is a composition, which is here to see how I am standing before God our Lord, and of the Angels and of the Saints interceding for me.
Second Prelude. The second, to ask for what I want. It will be here to ask for interior knowledge of so great good received, in order that being entirely grateful, I may be able in all to love and serve His Divine Majesty.
First Point. The First Point is, to bring to memory the benefits received, of Creation, Redemption and particular gifts, pondering with much feeling how much God our Lord has done for me, and how much He has given me of what He has, and then the same Lord desires to give me Himself as much as He can, according to His Divine ordination.
And with this to reflect on myself, considering with much reason and justice, what I ought on my side to offer and give to His Divine Majesty, that is to say, everything that is mine, and myself with it, as one who makes an offering with much feeling:
Take, Lord, and receive all my liberty, my memory, my intellect, and all my will—all that I have and possess. Thou gave it to me: to Thee, Lord, I return it! All is Thine, dispose of it according to all Thy will. Give me Thy love and grace, for this is enough for me.
Second Point. The second, to look how God dwells in creatures, in the elements, giving them being, in the plants vegetating, in the animals feeling in them, in men giving them to understand: and so in me, giving me being, animating me, giving me sensation and making me to understand; likewise making a temple of me, being created to the likeness and image of His Divine Majesty; reflecting as much on myself in the way which is said in the first Point, or in another which I feel to be better. In the same manner will be done on each Point which follows.
Third Point. The third, to consider how God works and labors for me in all things created on the face of the earth—that is, behaves like one who labors—as in the heavens, elements, plants, fruits, cattle, etc., giving them being, preserving them, giving them vegetation and sensation, etc.
Then to reflect on myself.
Fourth Point. The fourth, to look how all the good things and gifts descend from above, as my poor power from the supreme and infinite power from above; and so justice, goodness, pity, mercy, etc.; as from the sun descend the rays, from the fountain the waters, etc.
Then to finish reflecting on myself, as has been said.
I will end with a Colloquy and an Our Father."

Saint Ignatius of Loyola
(1491–1556)
Spiritual Exercises

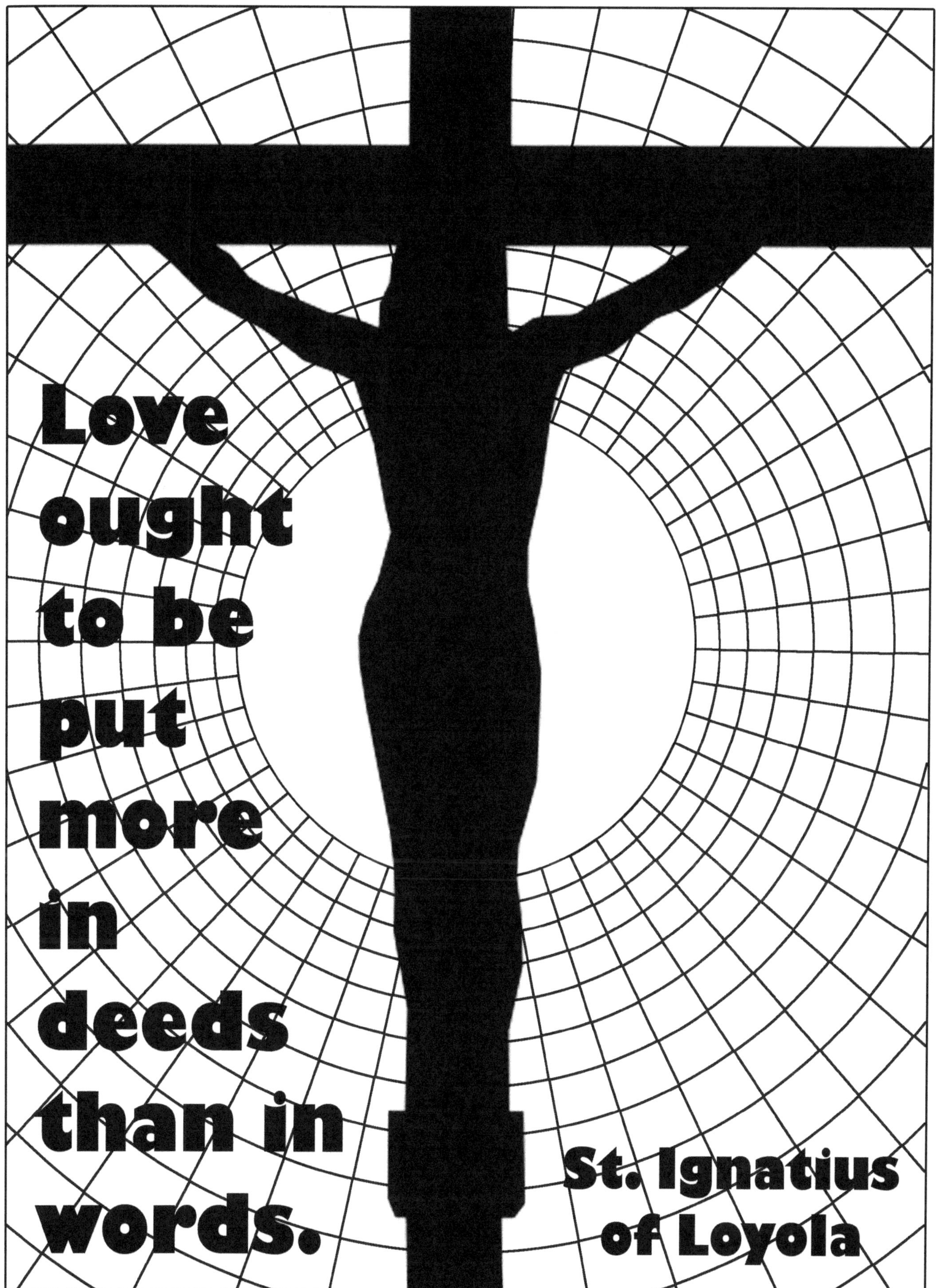
Love ought to be put more in deeds than in words.
St. Ignatius of Loyola

"Love is the most necessary of all virtues. Love in the person who preaches the word of God is like fire in a musket. If a person were to throw a bullet with his hands, he would hardly make a dent in anything; but if the person takes the same bullet and ignites some gunpowder behind it, it can kill. It is much the same with the word of God. If it is spoken by someone who is filled with the fire of charity—the fire of love of God and neighbor—it will work wonders."

Saint Anthony Mary Claret

Saint Anthony Mary Claret, C.M.F. (1807–1870) was a Spanish archbishop and missionary. He was the confessor of Queen Isabella II of Spain. He founded the Missionary Sons of the Immaculate Heart of Mary, also called the Claretians. He also founded some communities of religious sisters. The Claretians grew to over 450 houses with 3100 members with missions in five continents by the 21st century. He was active in charitable works, preaching, teaching, and he wrote over 144 books.

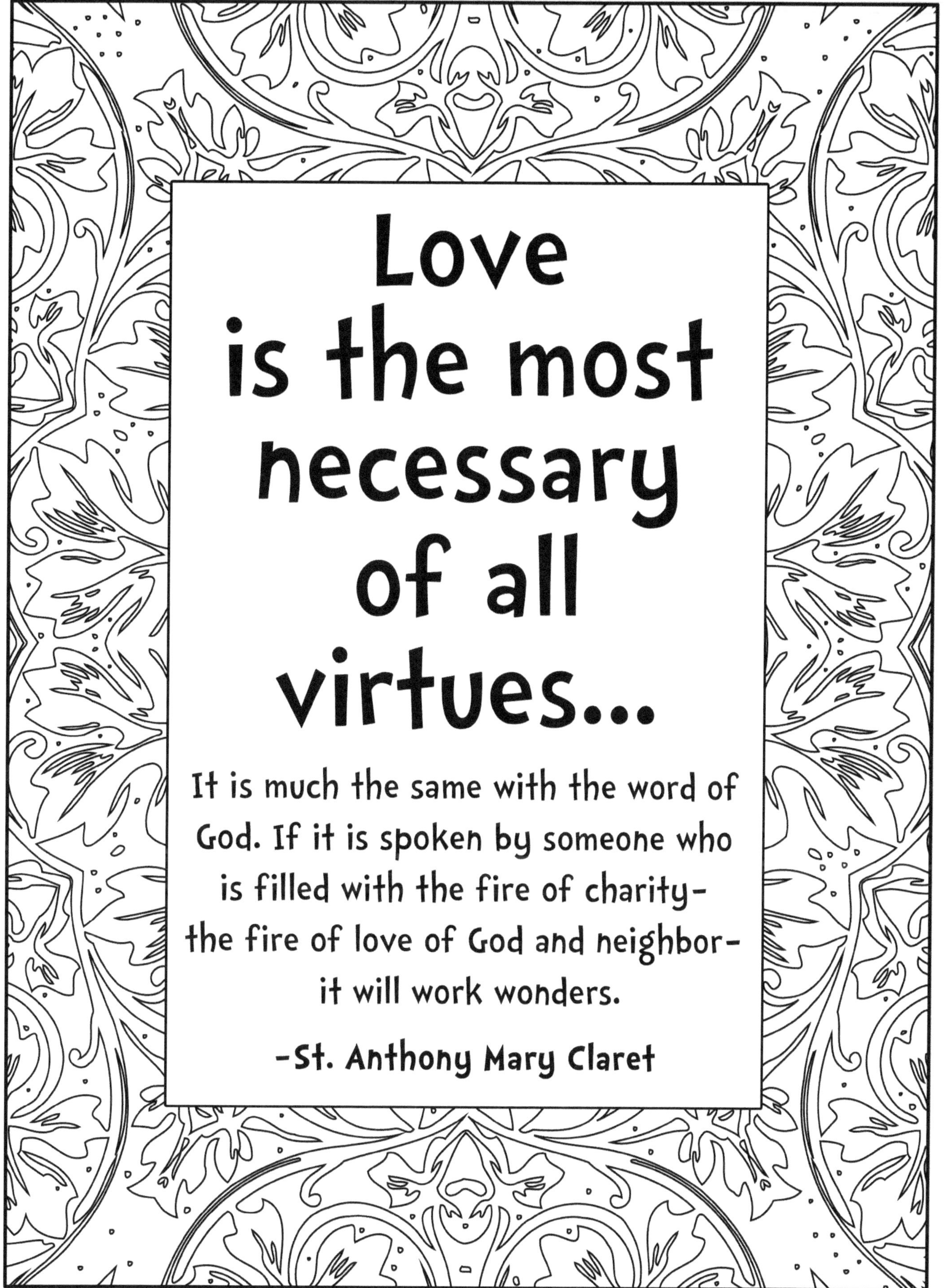
Love
is the most
necessary
of all
virtues...
It is much the same with the word of
God. If it is spoken by someone who
is filled with the fire of charity-
the fire of love of God and neighbor-
it will work wonders.
-St. Anthony Mary Claret

11 When I was a child, I used to talk as a child, think as a child, reason as a
child; when I became a man, I put aside childish things. 12 At present we see
indistinctly, as in a mirror, but then face to face. At present I know partially;
then I shall know fully, as I am fully known. 13 So faith, hope, love remain, these
three; but the greatest of these is love.

1 Corinthians 13:11-13
New American Bible, revised edition (NABRE)

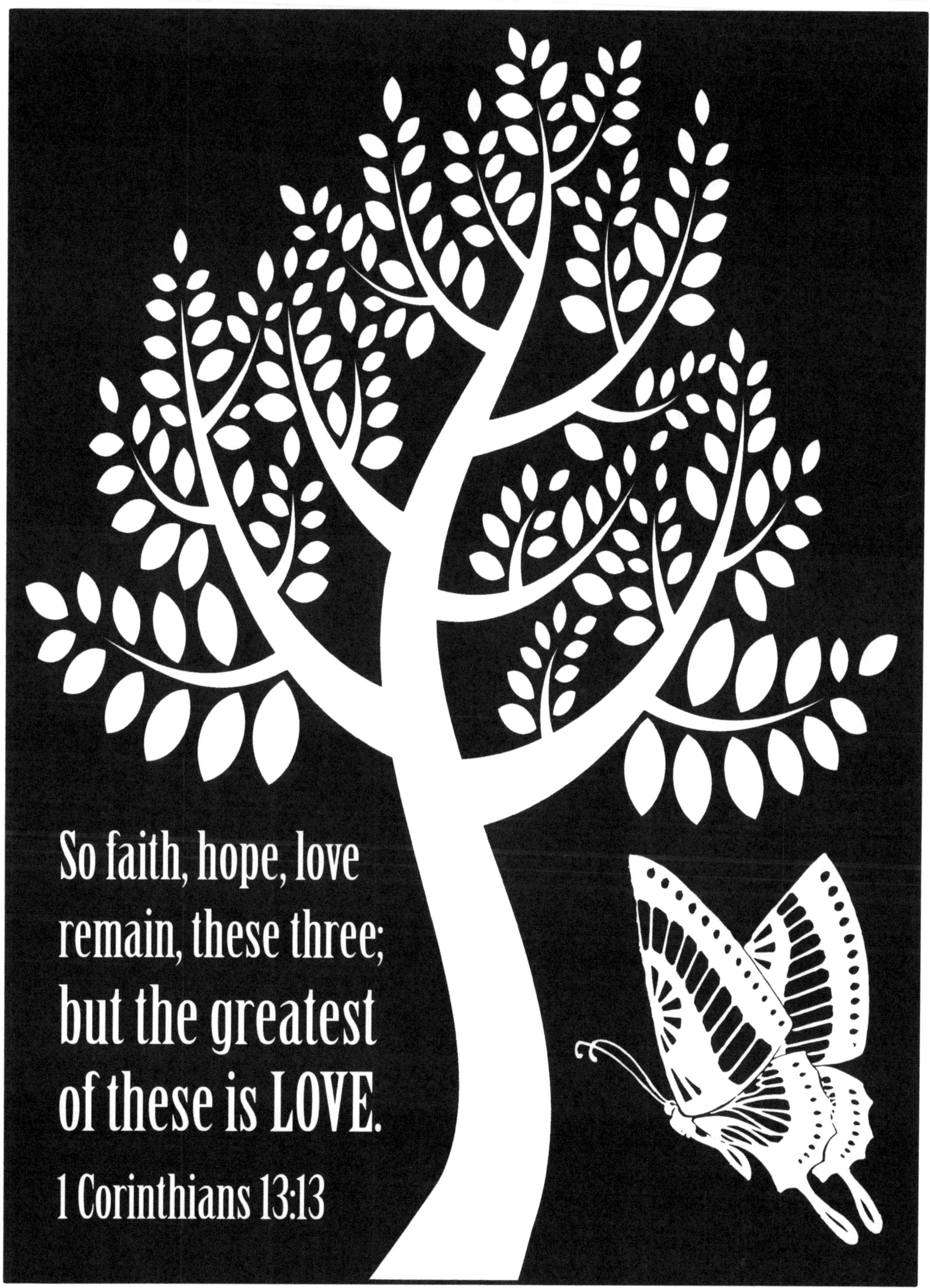
So faith, hope, love
remain, these three;
but the greatest
of these is LOVE.
1 Corinthians 13:13

12 This is my commandment: love one another as I love you. 13 No one has
greater love than this, to lay down one's life for one's friends. 14 You are my
friends if you do what I command you. 15 I no longer call you slaves, because a
slave does not know what his master is doing. I have called you friends,
because I have told you everything I have heard from my Father. 16 It was not
you who chose me, but I who chose you and appointed you to go and bear fruit
that will remain, so that whatever you ask the Father in my name he may give
you. 17 This I command you: love one another.

John 15:12-17
New American Bible, revised edition (NABRE)
⇨

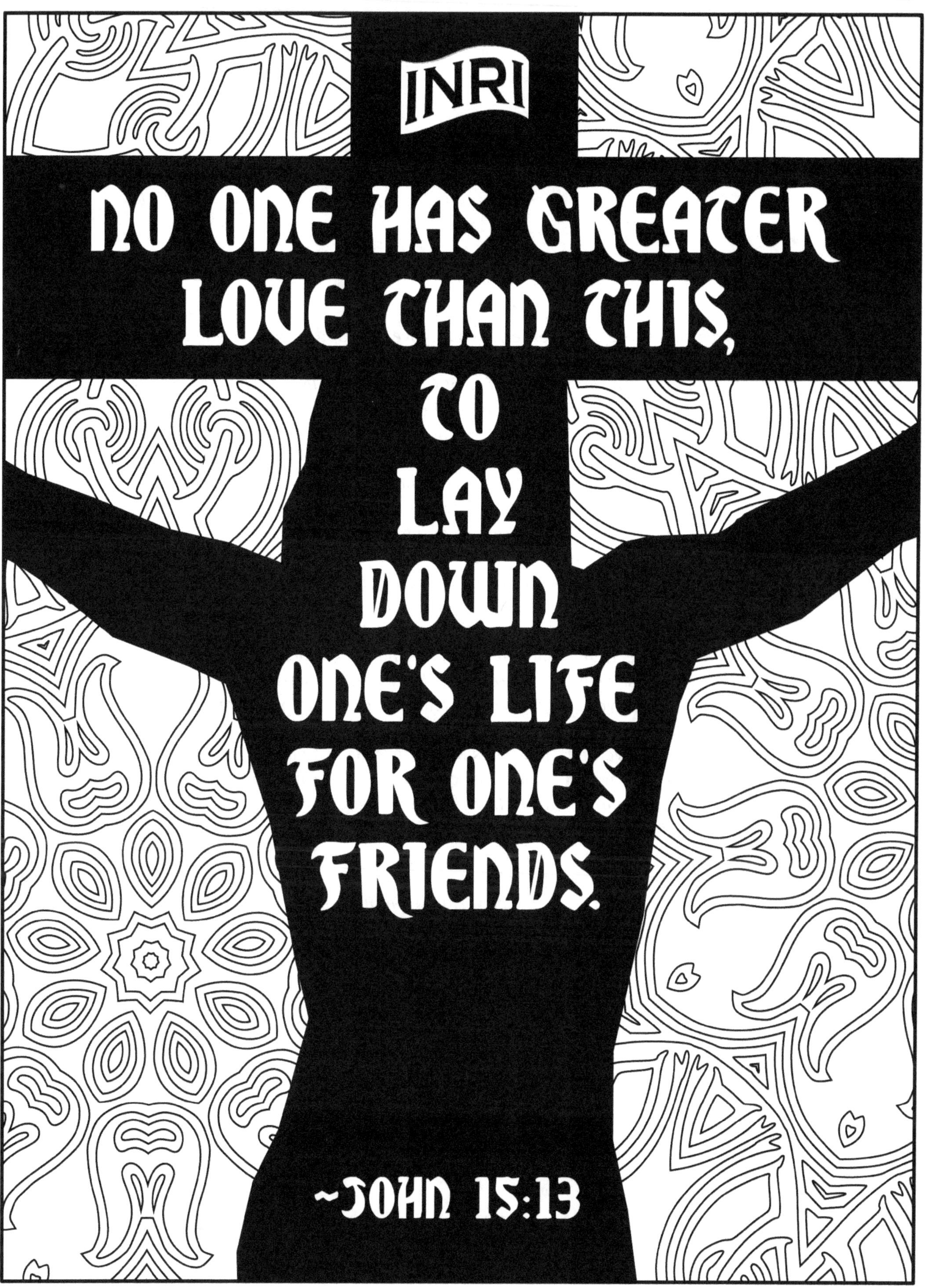
INRI
NO ONE HAS GREATER
LOVE THAN THIS,
TO
LAY
DOWN
ONE'S LIFE
FOR ONE'S
FRIENDS.
~JOHN 15:13

7 Beloved, let us love one another, because love is of God; everyone who loves is
begotten by God and knows God. 8 Whoever is without love does not know God,
for God is love. 9 In this way the love of God was revealed to us: God sent his
only Son into the world so that we might have life through him. 10 In this is love:
not that we have loved God, but that he loved us and sent his Son as expiation
for our sins. 11 Beloved, if God so loved us, we also must love one another. 12 No
one has ever seen God. Yet, if we love one another, God remains in us, and his
love is brought to perfection in us. 13 This is how we know that we remain in
him and he in us, that he has given us of his Spirit. 14 Moreover, we have seen
and testify that the Father sent his Son as savior of the world. 15 Whoever
acknowledges that Jesus is the Son of God, God remains in him and he in God.
16 We have come to know and to believe in the love God has for us. God is love,
and whoever remains in love remains in God and God in him. 17 In this is love
brought to perfection among us, that we have confidence on the day of
judgment because as he is, so are we in this world. 18 There is no fear in love,
but perfect love drives out fear because fear has to do with punishment, and so
one who fears is not yet perfect in love. 19 We love because he first loved us. 20 If
anyone says, "I love God," but hates his brother, he is a liar; for whoever does
not love a brother whom he has seen cannot love God whom he has not seen.
21 This is the commandment we have from him: whoever loves God must also
love his brother.

I John 4:7-21
New American Bible, revised edition (NABRE)

⇨

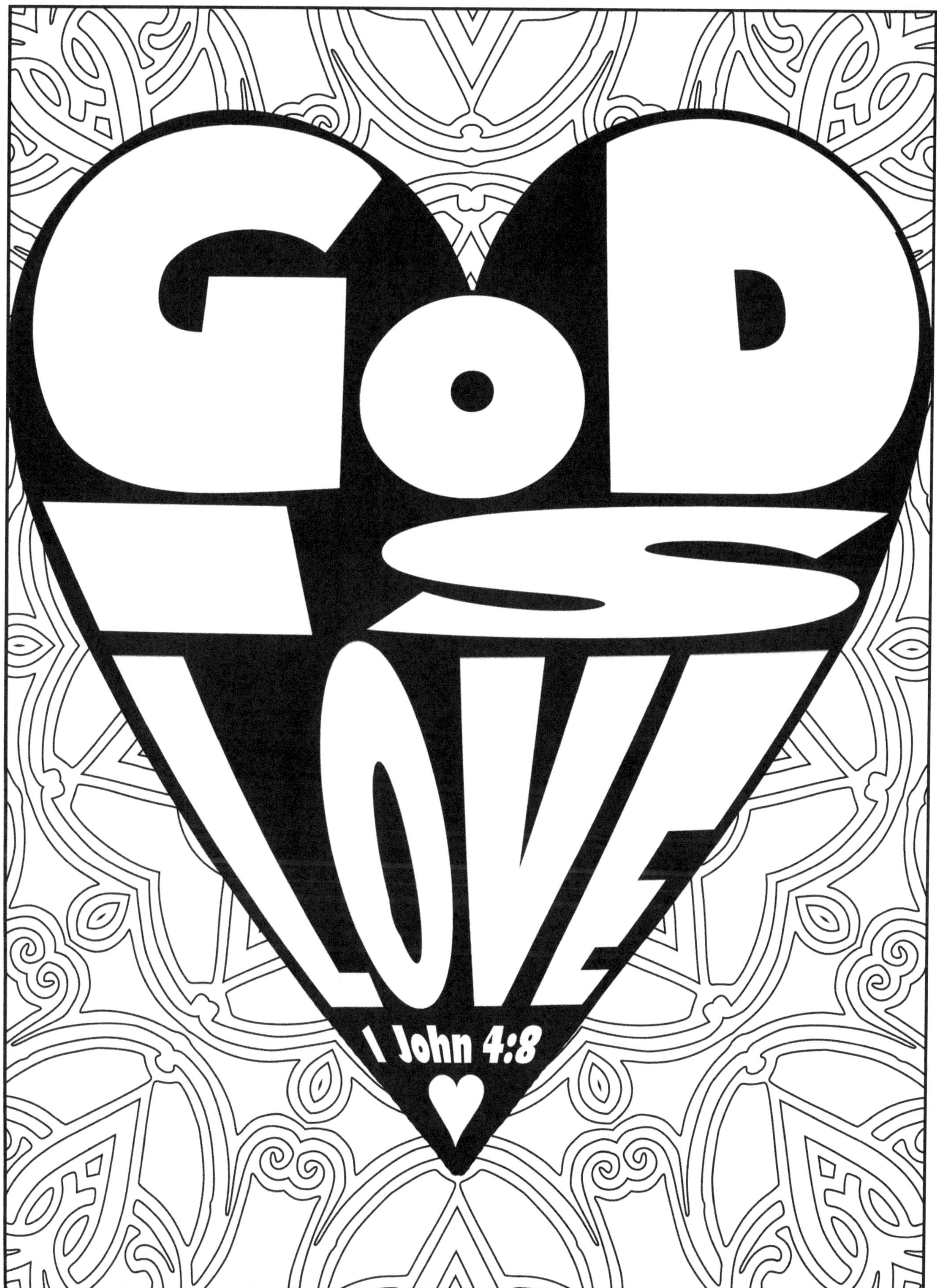
GOD
IS
LOVE
1 John 4:8

Note Cards to Color

The following pages have note cards to color using designs similar to the previous pages. For each card, cut on the solid line to the left and fold the card two times (into fourths) so that the picture is on the front of the card as shown below.

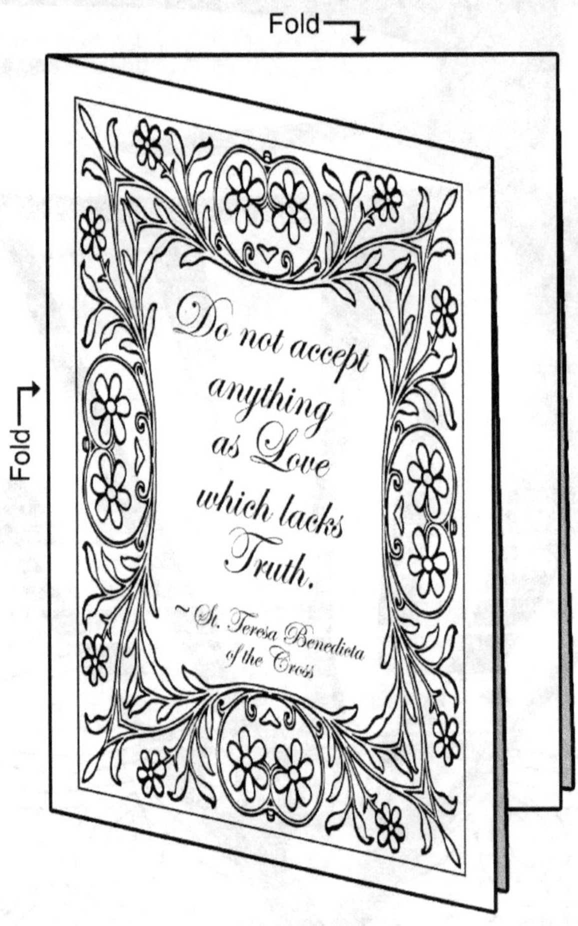

NOTE CARD TO COLOR: CUT ON THE LINE, AND THEN FOLD INTO 4THS WITH DESIGN ON FRONT OF CARD

A soul enkindled with love is a gentle, meek, humble and patient soul.

St. John of the Cross, OCD

NOTE CARD TO COLOR: CUT ON THE LINE, AND THEN FOLD INTO 4THS WITH DESIGN ON FRONT OF CARD

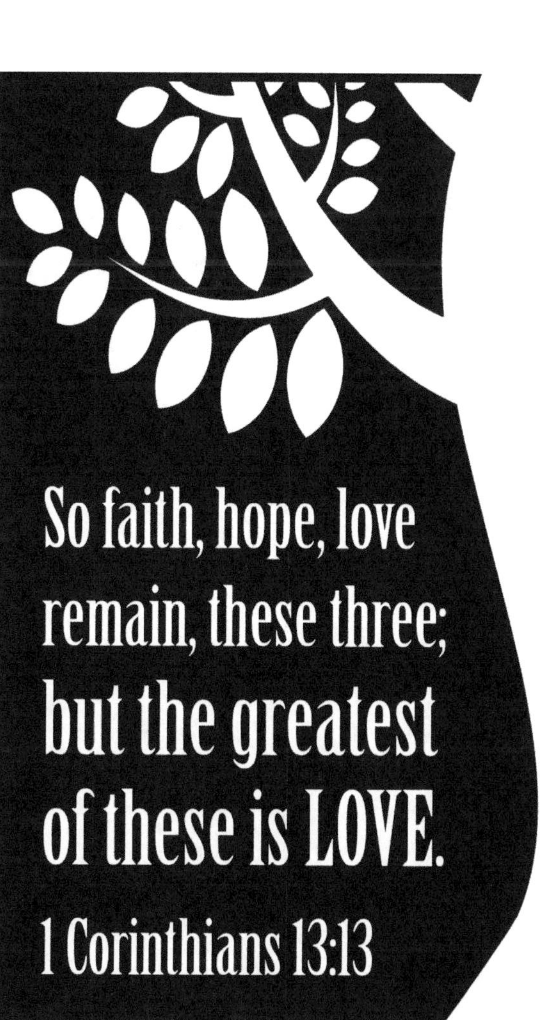

NOTE CARD TO COLOR: CUT ON THE LINE, AND THEN FOLD INTO 4THS WITH DESIGN ON FRONT OF CARD

A soul enkindled with love is a gentle, meek, humble and patient soul.

St. John of the Cross, OCD

NOTE CARD TO COLOR: CUT ON THE LINE, AND THEN FOLD INTO 4THS WITH DESIGN ON FRONT OF CARD

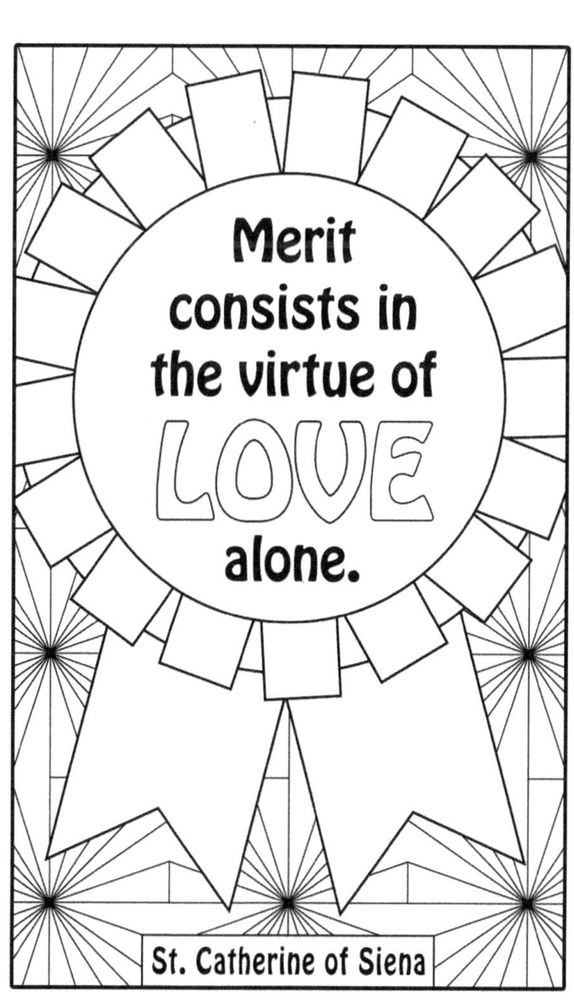

NOTE CARD TO COLOR: CUT ON THE LINE, AND THEN FOLD INTO 4THS WITH DESIGN ON FRONT OF CARD

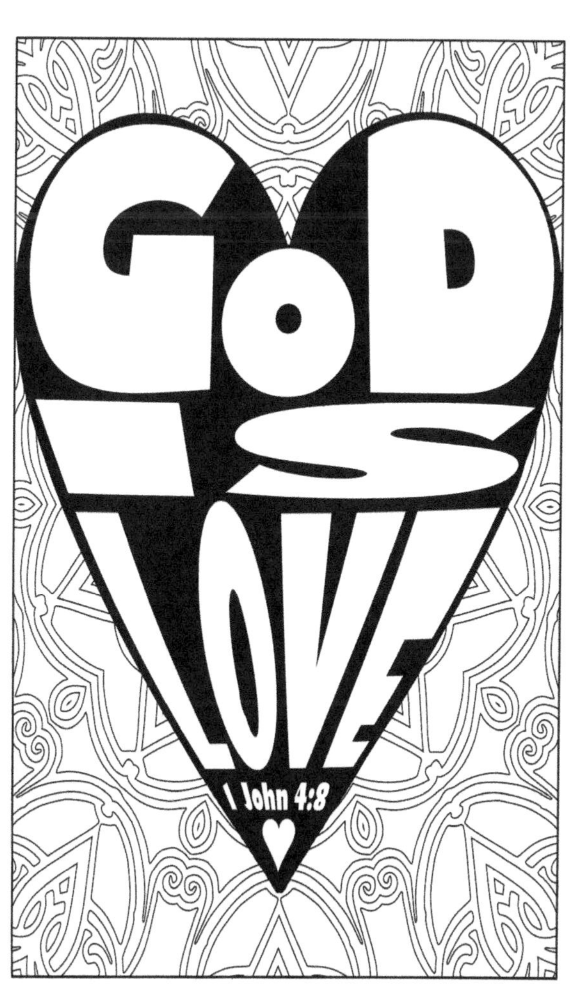

NOTE CARD TO COLOR: CUT ON THE LINE, AND THEN FOLD INTO 4THS WITH DESIGN ON FRONT OF CARD

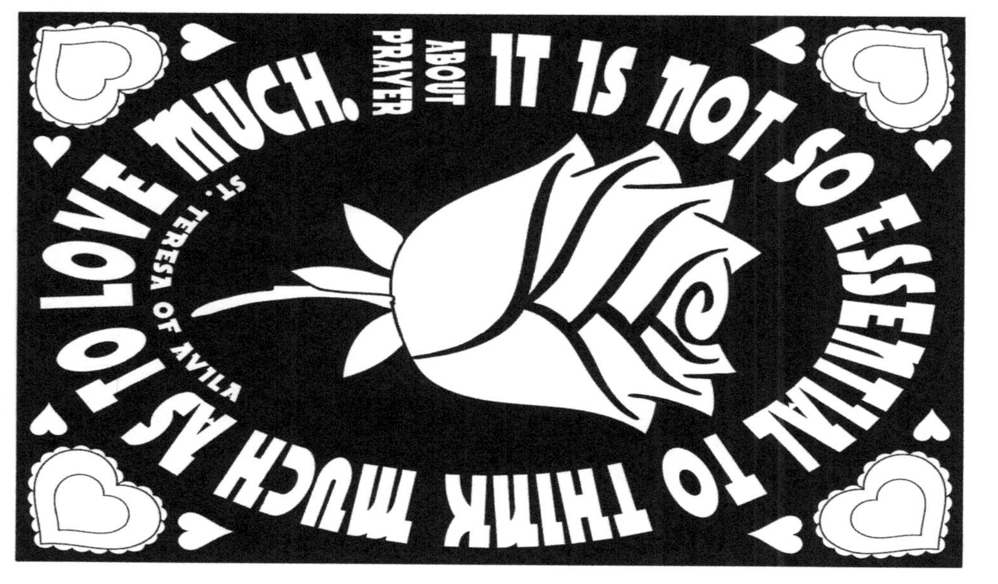

NOTE CARD TO COLOR: CUT ON THE LINE, AND THEN FOLD INTO 4THS WITH DESIGN ON FRONT OF CARD

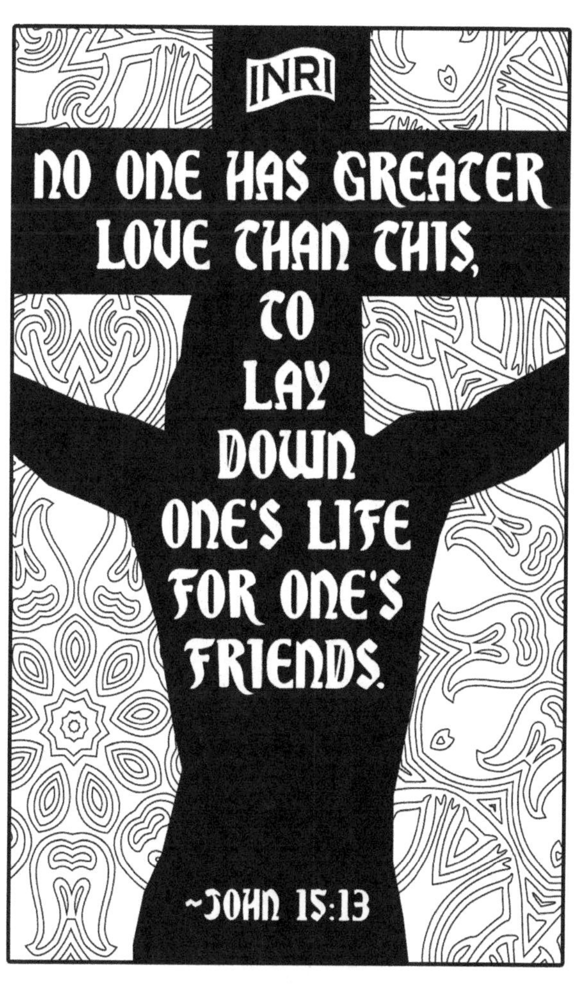

NOTE CARD TO COLOR: CUT ON THE LINE, AND THEN FOLD INTO 4THS WITH DESIGN ON FRONT OF CARD

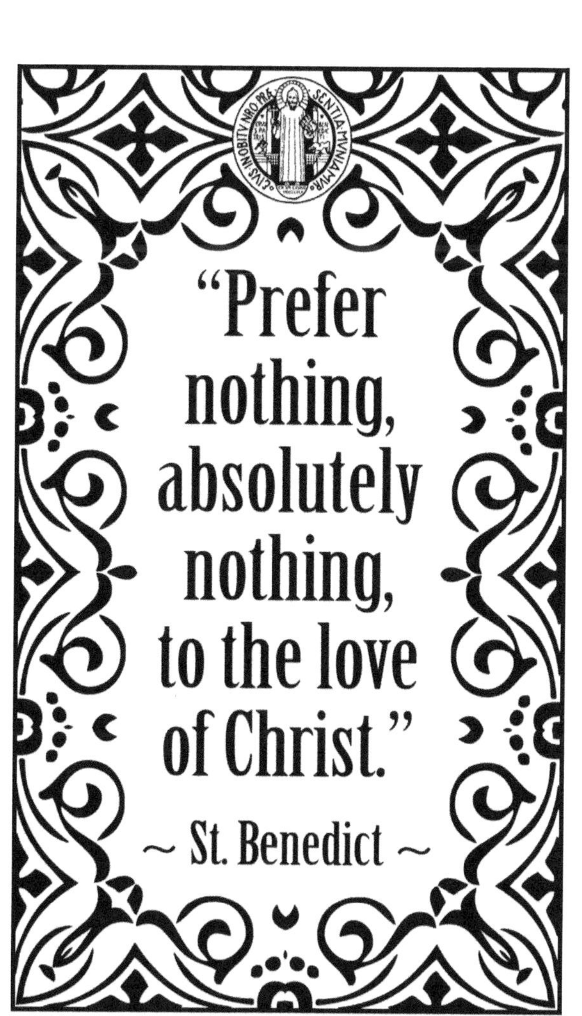

NOTE CARD TO COLOR: CUT ON THE LINE, AND THEN FOLD INTO 4THS WITH DESIGN ON FRONT OF CARD

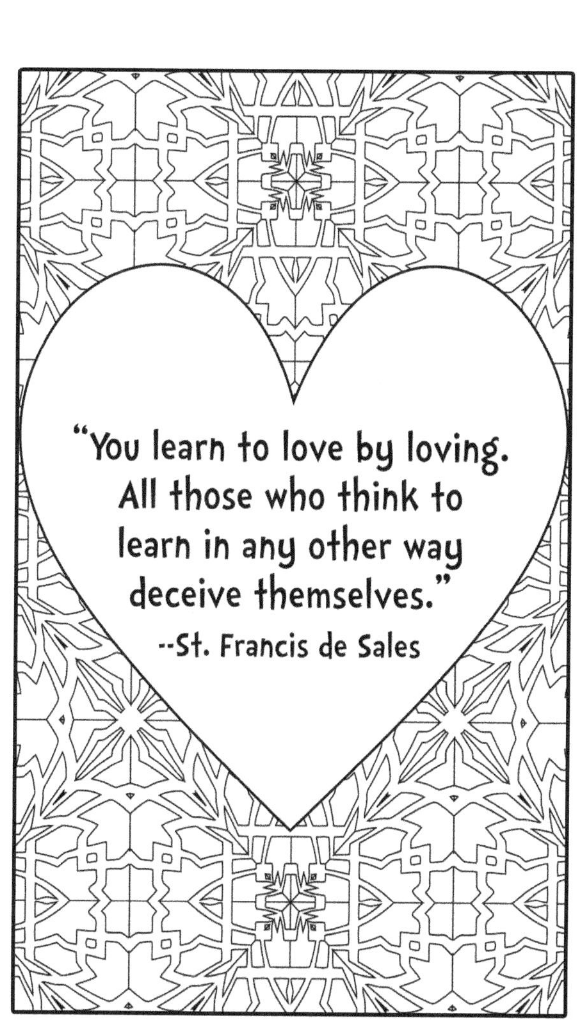

NOTE CARD TO COLOR: CUT ON THE LINE, AND THEN FOLD INTO 4THS WITH DESIGN ON FRONT OF CARD

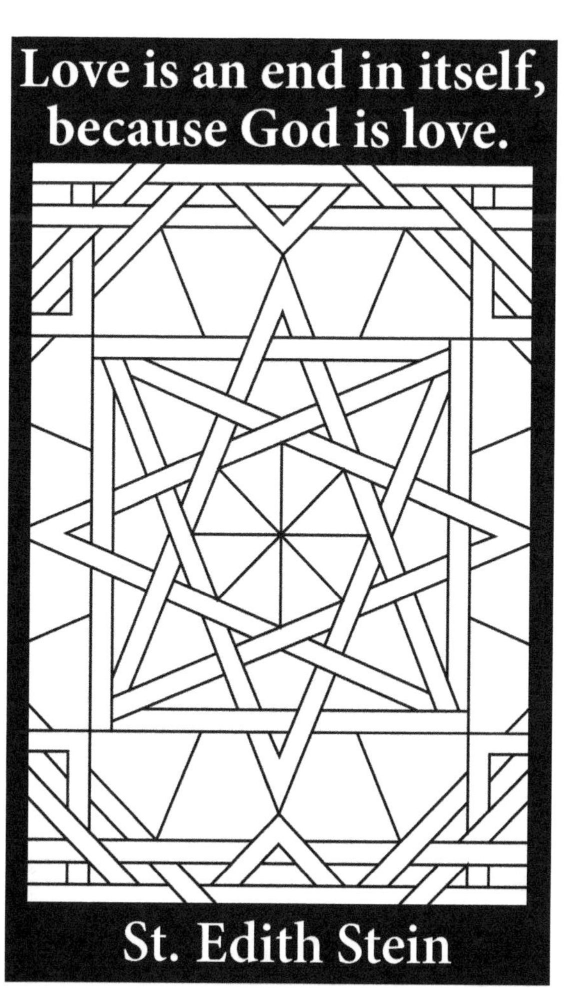

NOTE CARD TO COLOR: CUT ON THE LINE, AND THEN FOLD INTO 4THS WITH DESIGN ON FRONT OF CARD

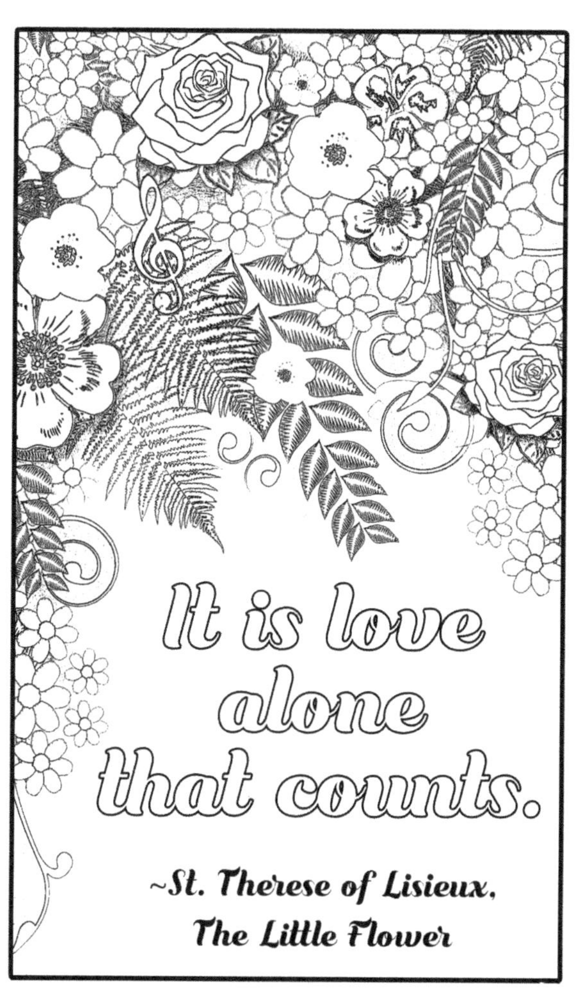

NOTE CARD TO COLOR: CUT ON THE LINE, AND THEN FOLD INTO 4THS WITH DESIGN ON FRONT OF CARD

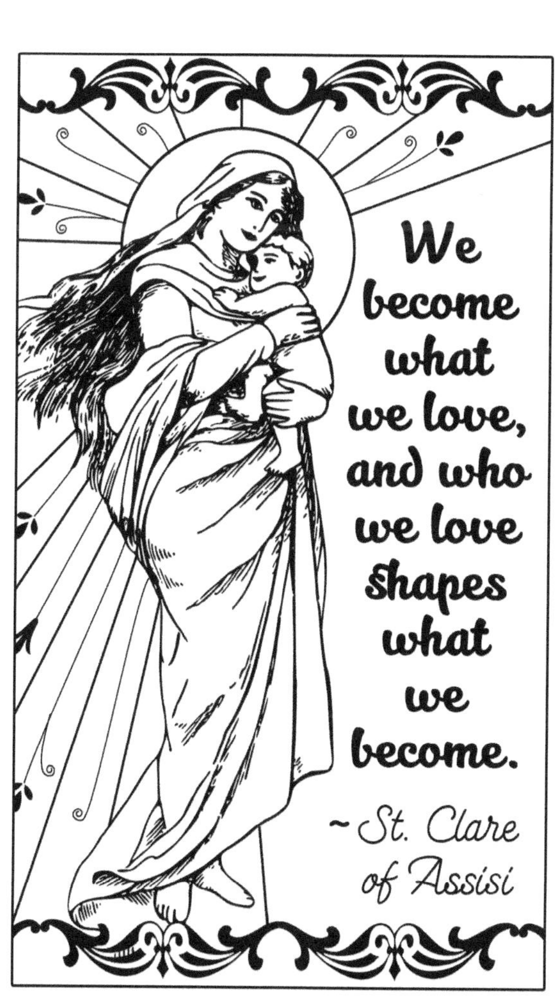

NOTE CARD TO COLOR: CUT ON THE LINE, AND THEN FOLD INTO 4THS WITH DESIGN ON FRONT OF CARD

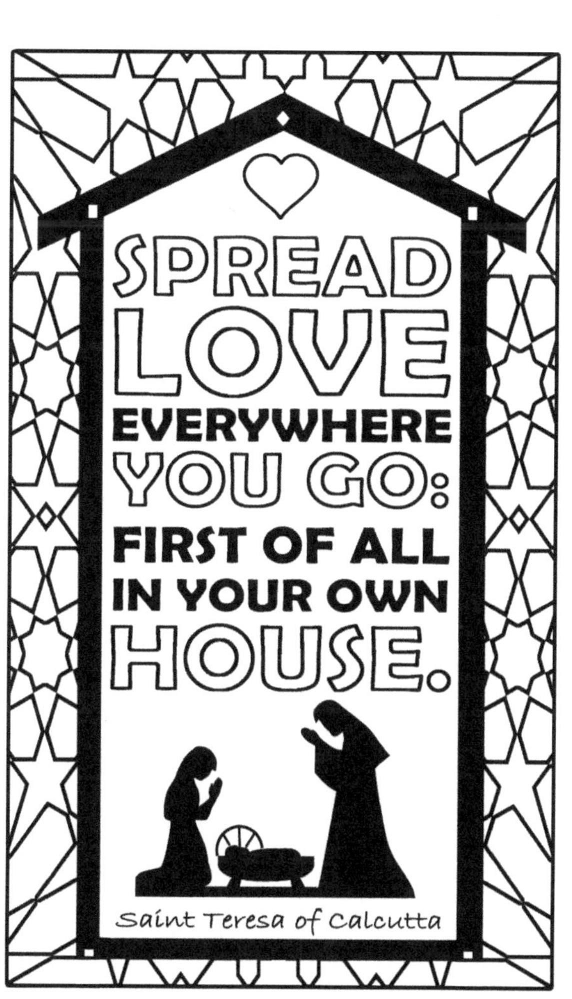

NOTE CARD TO COLOR: CUT ON THE LINE, AND THEN FOLD INTO 4THS WITH DESIGN ON FRONT OF CARD

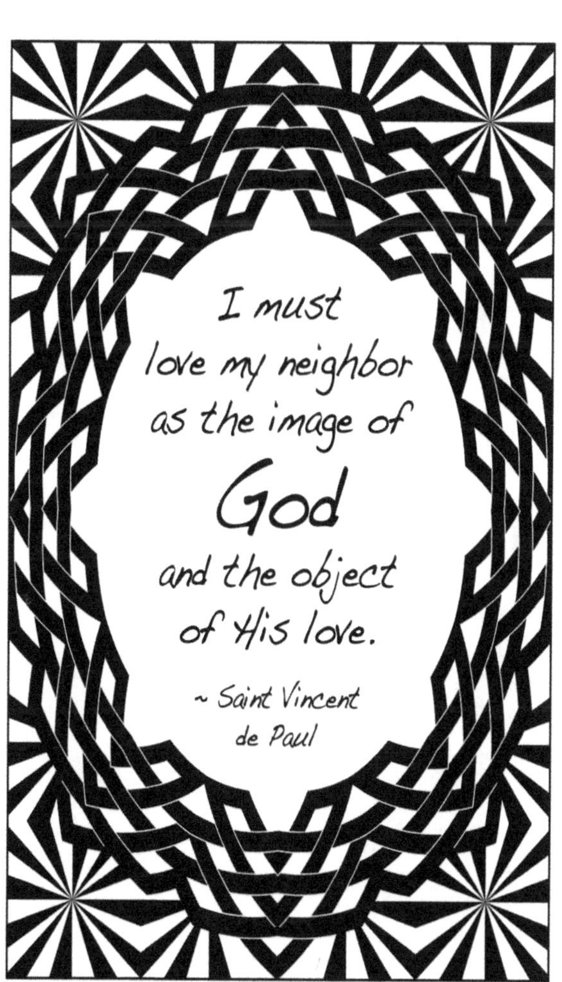

NOTE CARD TO COLOR: CUT ON THE LINE, AND THEN FOLD INTO 4THS WITH DESIGN ON FRONT OF CARD

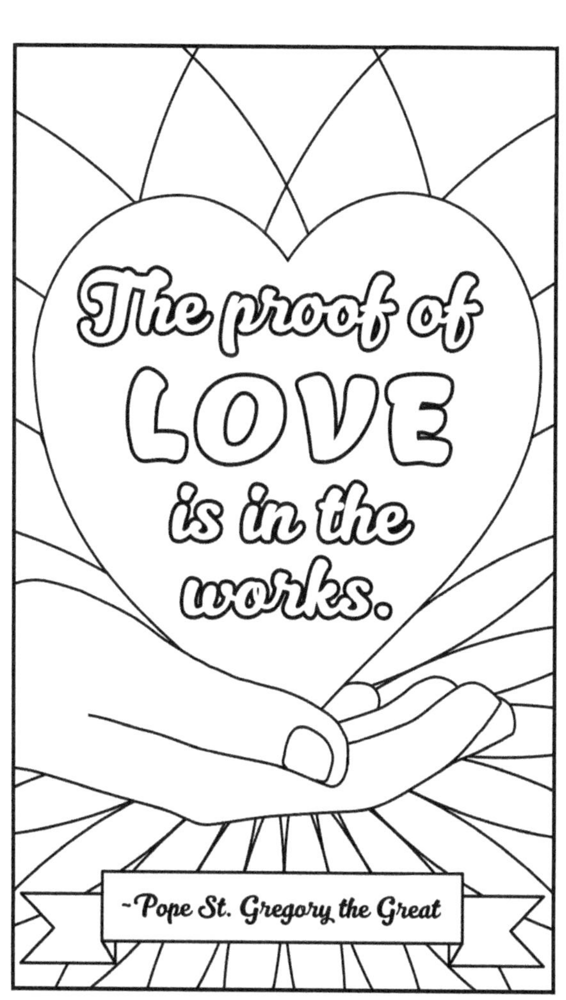

NOTE CARD TO COLOR: CUT ON THE LINE, AND THEN FOLD INTO 4THS WITH DESIGN ON FRONT OF CARD

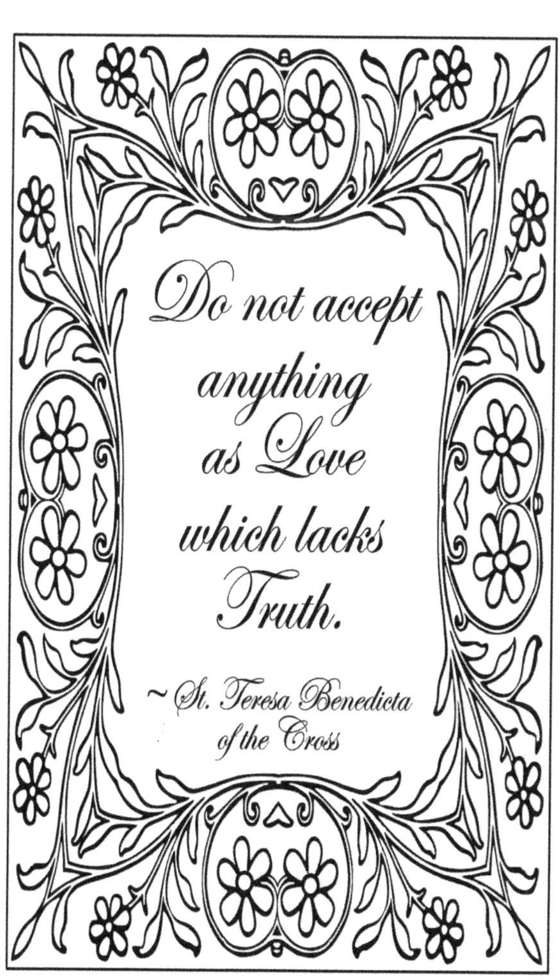

NOTE CARD TO COLOR: CUT ON THE LINE, AND THEN FOLD INTO 4THS WITH DESIGN ON FRONT OF CARD

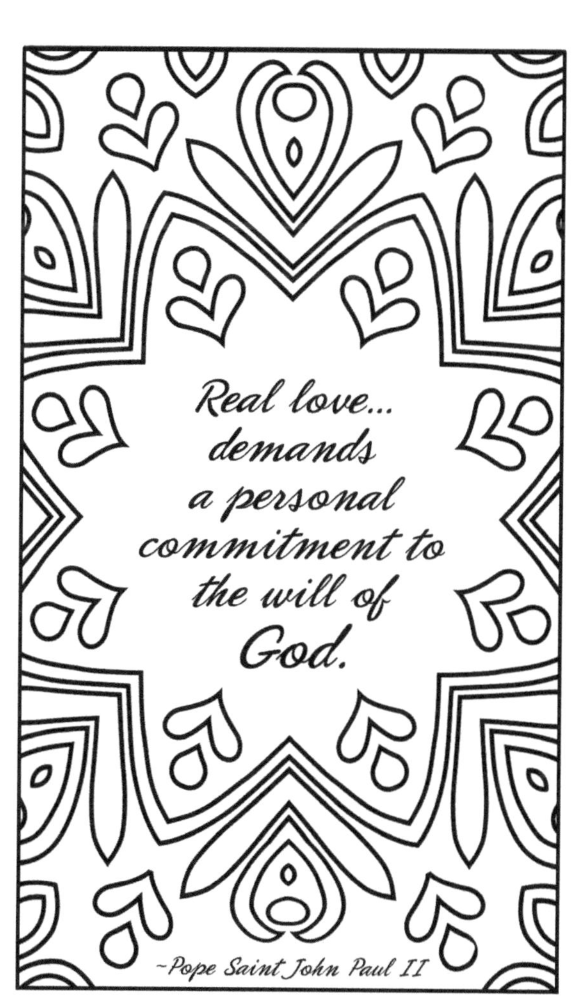

NOTE CARD TO COLOR: CUT ON THE LINE, AND THEN FOLD INTO 4THS WITH DESIGN ON FRONT OF CARD

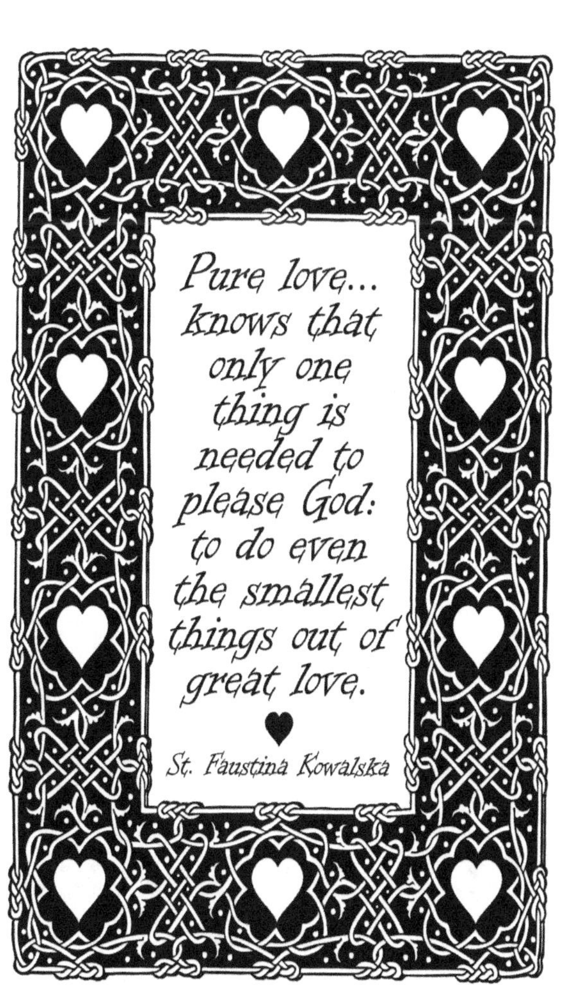

NOTE CARD TO COLOR: CUT ON THE LINE, AND THEN FOLD INTO 4THS WITH DESIGN ON FRONT OF CARD

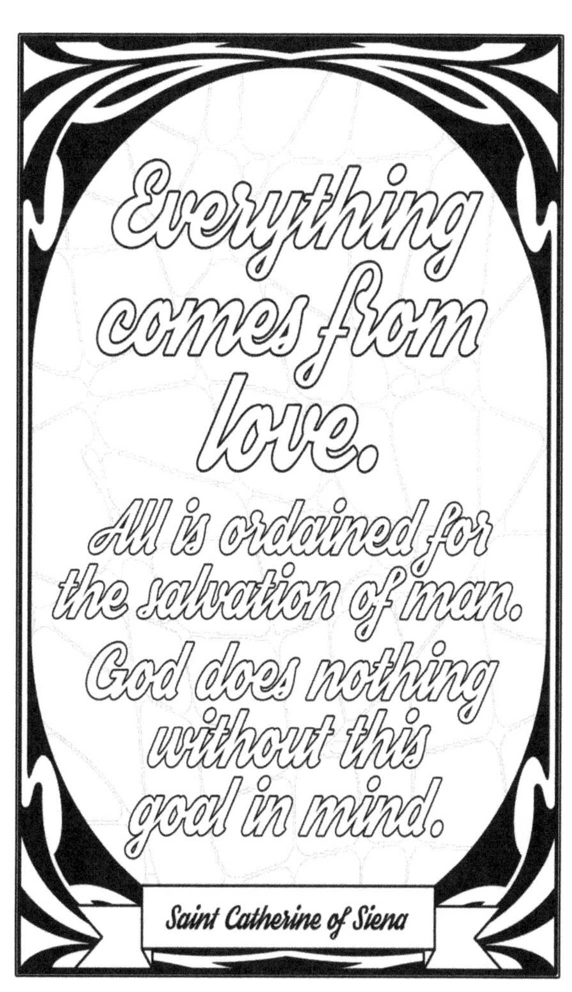

NOTE CARD TO COLOR: CUT ON THE LINE, AND THEN FOLD INTO 4THS WITH DESIGN ON FRONT OF CARD

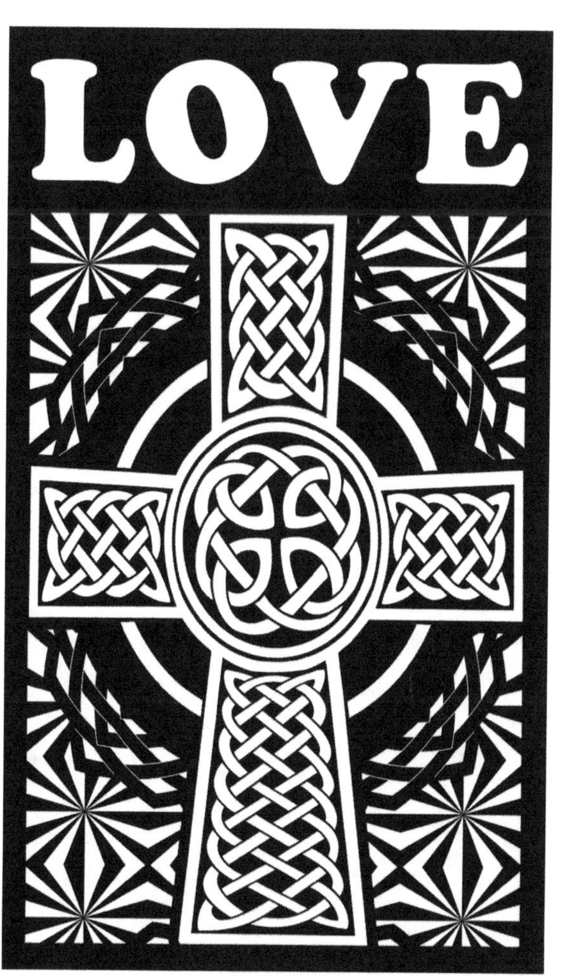

NOTE CARD TO COLOR: CUT ON THE LINE, AND THEN FOLD INTO 4THS WITH DESIGN ON FRONT OF CARD

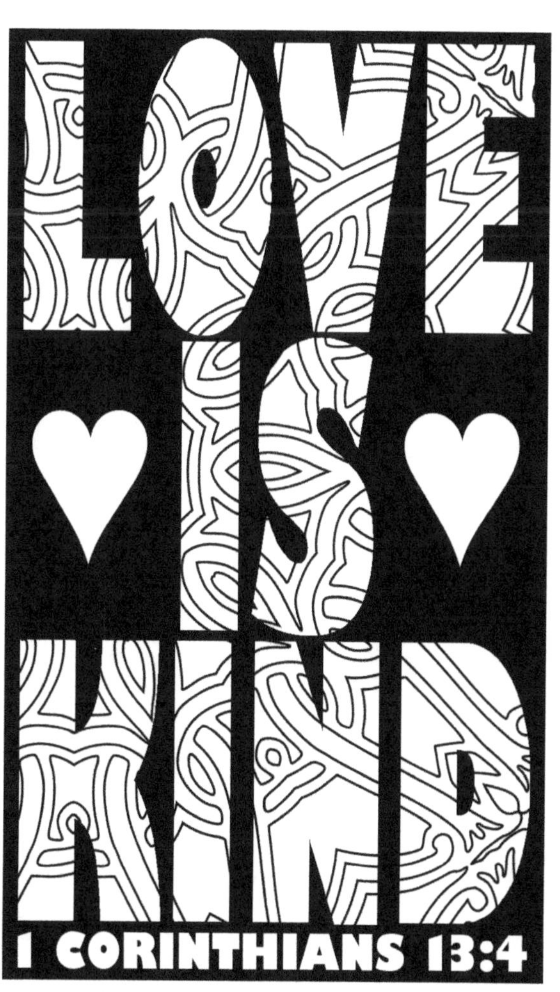

NOTE CARD TO COLOR: CUT ON THE LINE, AND THEN FOLD INTO 4THS WITH DESIGN ON FRONT OF CARD

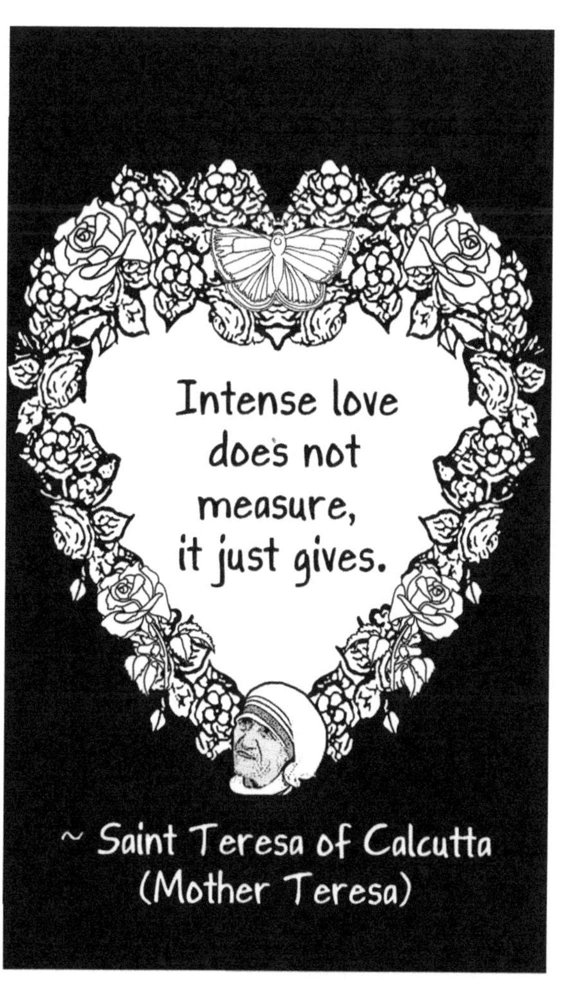

NOTE CARD TO COLOR: CUT ON THE LINE, AND THEN FOLD INTO 4THS WITH DESIGN ON FRONT OF CARD

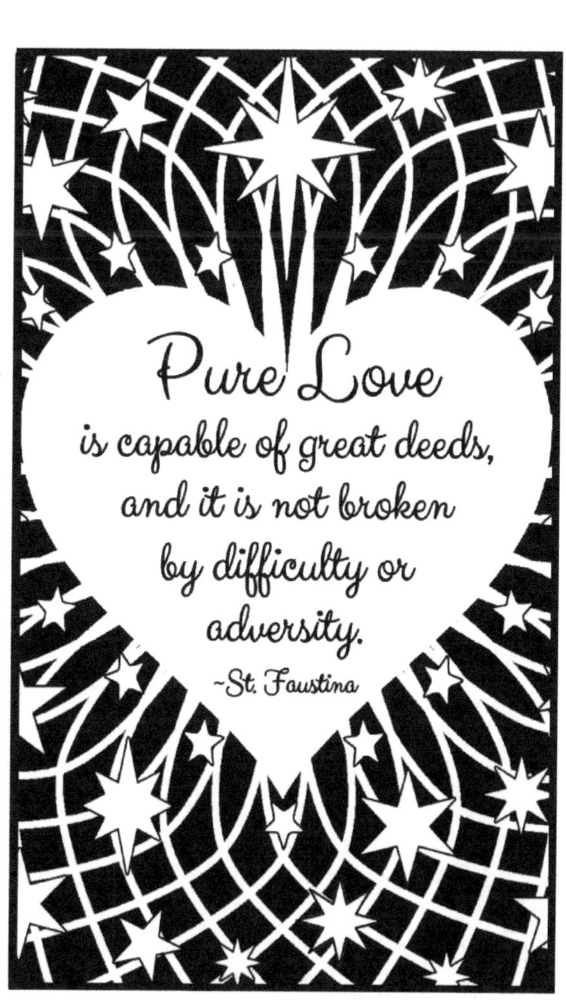

www.ingramcontent.com/pod-product-compliance
Lightning Source LLC
LaVergne TN
LVHW081614110826
845155LV00039BA/191

9781944158033